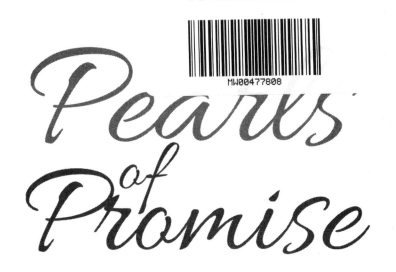

Pearls of Promise

*A devotional designed to
reassure you of God's love.*

KUDU

compiled and edited by

LISA BURKHARDT WORLEY
LISA MICK
CATHERINE WEISKOPF

Pearls of Promise: A Devotional Designed to Reassure You of God's Love
edited by Lisa Burkhardt Worley, Lisa Mick, Catherine Weiskopf

copyright 2013 Lisa Burkhardt Worley, Lisa Mick, Catherine Weiskopf

trade paperback ISBN: 9781938624445
ebook ISBN: 9781938624452

Pearls of Promise is also available on Amazon Kindle, Apple iBooks and Barnes & Noble Nook formats.

Cover art and section divider art by Kelly LaFarge. Kelly has worked in art and design for over thirty years. She is proud to be one of many great women doing great things for God. See her work at *kellylafarge.net*

We would like to thank our Lord for bringing our team together and dedicate this devotional to Him first, then to the pearls in our lives—family and friends—who have been instruments of support, grace, and love.

— Lisa W., Cathy, and Lisa M.

Introduction

When you wear a string of pearls have you ever thought about what it took to create the beautiful round shapes that make up your necklace?

A natural pearl begins its life inside an oyster's shell when an intruder, such as a grain of sand or bit of floating food, slips in between one of the two shells. In order to protect itself from irritation, the oyster will quickly begin covering the uninvited visitor with layers of nacre, the mineral substance that creates the mollusk's shells. The nacre, also known as mother-of-pearl, coats the grain of sand until the iridescent gem is formed.

In the same way, God creates a pearl out of every trial or struggle in our lives. How many pearls has He produced in your life? I am sure I have enough to string together many pearl necklaces!

That's why our ministry is called "Pearls of Promise." Each of the members of our Pearls Team have experienced many trials in life that God has turned around for good, and we believe everyone has a story that God has transformed into a pearl.

The *Pearls of Promise* devotional shares pearls from the lives of forty-six different writers from across the country, life experiences we hope will encourage millions of women. The book is structured in a way that women can go directly to the "Pearl" they are yearning for. The pearls are inspirationally deep and hopefully provide a connection to God.

I attended a writing seminar where the speaker said, "Truth is taught only by experience, which is best delivered through well-told stories." The *Pearls of Promise* devotional is full of well-told stories that deliver truth.

What does the Bible say about pearls? There are several references but my favorite is in Matthew 13:45. It says, *Again, the kingdom of heaven is like a merchant looking for fine pearls. When he found one of great value, he went away and sold everything he had and bought it.*

It is our hope there is a slice of heaven in each of these devotions in the *Pearls of Promise* devotional. Each of these authors have seen God's hand in their lives and have claimed the pearls He has produced through their life experiences. We hope the stories shared will provide you with a beautiful pearl necklace for encouragement as you learn how the Lord created something of great value in the lives of others.

Lisa Burkhardt Worley
Founder, Pearls of Promise Ministries

Contents

Pearls of Encouragement

Pearls of Faith

Pearls of Comfort

Pearls of Praise

Pearls of Prayer

Pearls of Love

Pearls of Joy

Pearls of Peace

Pearls of Forgiveness

Pearls of Trust

Pearls of Truth

Pearls of Wisdom

Pearls of Encouragement

What Jesus Worked for Good at Columbine

Beth Shriver

*P*raise be to the God and Father of our Lord Jesus Christ, the Father of compassion and the God of all comfort, who comforts us in all our troubles, so that we can comfort those in any trouble with the comfort we ourselves have received from God *(2 Corinthians 1:3-4).*

My children were five and seven at the time of the Columbine shooting. Their elementary school was where students reunited with their parents. Our babysitter, who was a student there, hid under a table in the cafeteria for hours until the SWAT team came. She later spoke to schools with the message, *"Where would you be in your faith if that happened to you today?"* Her calling was just one of the many *What Jesus works for good* that came from that tragedy.

The community created a network of people willing to help those in need. From counselors to hall monitors, prayer walks, and more, people stepped up and did their part. *What Jesus works for good.*

Church groups helped with meals. Usually a simple task, but delivering meals to those who had lost a child or had an injured child was not simple at all. Many broke down at the sight of us when we came bearing home cooked meals. *What Jesus works for good.*

14

A mother whose son was injured started a prevention committee. She didn't pity herself having a son who would never have the use of his leg. She got involved like the rest of us. *What Jesus works for good.*

Our good friend was on the SWAT team that day. He wouldn't talk about his experience buried in his heavy heart. But because of his experience, he created new strategies and nationwide training for other SWAT teams on how to deal with situations like Columbine. *What Jesus works for good.*

Our neighbor was in the science room, hiding in a closet with another student and a teacher who had been shot and had died during her watch. She had a difficult time recovering from that experience, but she became a believer through it all. *What Jesus works for good.*

The Olympics reminded our country of Columbine when the principal of the school ran with the torch down the street in front of Columbine High School. He is still the principal today. *What Jesus works for good.*

Count them, seven—the perfect number—works for good. One horrific day against an infinity of what Christ is still working for good.

Faith Step: How will you let Jesus heal you through your struggles?

Beth Shriver is the author of *Annie's Truth, Grace Given* and *Healing Grace.* Her website is *BethShriverWriter.com.*

Dirty Laundry

Lisa Burkhardt Worley

My dryer broke last week. Those of you who have lots of dirty laundry know what that means. For a while my house looked like a clothing museum with blouses and shorts hanging on every available hook trying to air dry!

But no matter how hard I tried, the dirty laundry kept piling up. It was overwhelming. Even when the dryer was finally repaired, it still seemed like an endless process. If only someone would clean up my dirty laundry for me!

Isn't that the way it is with our lives? We have so many baskets of dirty laundry in our past we don't think they could ever be cleaned up. We have secret sins that no one knows about, and we figure if they did, they might think less of us. Our knowledge of our sin prevents us from having a vibrant relationship with God because we think there's too much to overcome. How could He ever forgive a wretch like me?

Good News! God has a washer and dryer that can handle all of our dirty laundry! We may think we've stuffed it away in our closet so no one can see the mounds of filth in our lives, but we cannot hide anything from God. He is ready and willing to take our past and launder it for us. 1 John 1:9 says, *If we confess our sins, He is faithful and just and will forgive us our sins and purify us from all unrighteousness.*

That means all sins, even the most soiled garment you have.

While we often have trouble forgiving ourselves,

God desires to forgive us. All He wants is for us to turn the dirty laundry over to Him.

The Israelites had the same problem. They had a nation full of dirty laundry, but God loved them so much He wanted them to repent and be restored. In Isaiah 1:18-20 He laid it out for them:

Come now, let us reason together, says the Lord. Though your sins are like scarlet, they shall be as white as snow; though they are red as crimson, they shall be like wool. If you are willing and obedient, you will eat the best from the land; but if you resist and rebel, you will be devoured by the sword.

Through this passage, God is also telling us to be reasonable. He doesn't want our dirty laundry weighing us down. All we have to do is give Him all of our life, not just the good parts, so He can help us keep our laundry clean in the future.

Are you willing to hand over your dirty laundry?

Lisa Burkhardt Worley is a former national television sports reporter, now Christian motivational speaker and writer and is the founder of Pearls of Promise Ministries, *pearlsofpromiseministries.com.* She is the co-author of the award winning manuscript, *If I Only Had...Following God's Path to Your Security* and is co-authoring a new Bible study about how God takes you out of the world to do the unpopular. Lisa is also an editor for the *Pearls of Promise* devotional.

Grandma, You Did It!

Cathy Biggerstaff

My four-year-old granddaughter Emma phoned me to ask if I would like to go on a field trip with her. The class trip would fall on a day when Mommy would be out of town. I quickly accepted her invitation, not caring where they were going. My fun would come from sharing the day with Emma.

She spent the night with me on Thursday night and early Friday morning we left in time to get to her school by 8:30. I am directionally challenged, had never been to the school Emma attends in another city, and Emma knew I was tentative about the directions Mommy had given me. I put on my best face and pretended to be confident.

I breathed a sigh of relief when we pulled into the school parking lot on time and with only one minor wrong turn. As we unsnapped our seat belts, Emma burst out of her booster seat. With great expression, her beautiful eyes sparkling, and her arms waving in the air, she yelled out, "Grandma, you did it!"

It touched my heart to know that she had been pulling for me every mile of our journey that day. Once I accomplished the goal, she couldn't hold back her enthusiasm. We have raised her in an atmosphere of praise and encouragement and it naturally and easily poured out of her that morning.

I loved being on the receiving end of encouragement,

and even more so since it came from a four-year-old. I see great things in her future as she interacts with people and shows them how to be encouragers.

Are you an encourager? In 1 Thessalonians 5:11 we read, *Therefore encourage one another and build up each other, as indeed you are doing* (NKJV). This passage assumes we are already encouragers, but I know it doesn't come naturally to some people. The good news is you can train yourself to be one. Just keep your eyes and heart open to the people around you. When you see them doing a good thing, be generous with your praise and thanks.

Here are a few instances I've encountered just this week: a child drawing a picture, a lady with a beautiful smile, a clerk who took extra care to wrap a breakable item, a child who had just learned to tie his shoes, and a waiter who went above and beyond to see that my friend had a good birthday experience.

The opportunities are all around you. "You can do it!"

Cathy Biggerstaff, a Christian clown, blogs weekly at *cathybiggerstaff. blogspot.com* and would love for you to visit and follow her Joyful Journey. She writes children's books, curriculum, and devotionals. Cathy is published in *Mature Living Magazine,* on *ChristianDevotions.us,* and she guest blogs.

The Polisher

Lisa Mick

Marriage reminds me of taking two rough rocks, placing them in a polisher and letting them rub together. When they emerge from the polisher they are smooth and beautiful, but only because they've spent time together removing all the rough, ugly spots. This polishing takes time, work, and constant mixing together.

I have been married for 25 years and have spent many years being corrected, ground, and improved by God. In my own marriage, we have been in the polisher many, many times. We keep starting again and again and are becoming stronger and smoother by staying the course.

The Lord gives us many lessons along the way. The choice is ours to either let Him do the sanding, grow and become stronger or jump out of the polisher and stop the process. If we stop the polishing process, we lose the blessing He has in store for our marriage.

One example of this polishing from our marriage was that a few years ago I had trouble accepting my husband for who he was. Frankly, I thought he was the one with all the rough spots. In response, the Lord showed me this passage: *Accept the one whose faith is weak, without quarreling over disputable matters. One person's faith allows them to eat anything, but another, whose faith is weak, eats only vegetables. The one who eats everything must not treat with contempt the one who does not, and the one who does not eat everything must not judge the one who does, for God has accepted them. Who are you to judge someone else's servant? To their own master, servants stand or fall. And they will stand, for the Lord is able to make them stand* (Romans 14:1-4).

This was an eye opener for me, because the Lord speaks to us through His Word and it says God has accepted him. Wow! Talk about spiritual discipline for me. Who am I? I can't make him stand but it says the Lord is able to do it. I asked forgiveness that day and set out to be put back in the polisher and let the Lord start another process. Today my husband and I are smoother and more beautiful than ever.

Lisa Mick is director of outreach for Pearls of Promise Ministries and is also one of the editors for the *Pearls of Promise* devotional. Lisa is also co-authoring a Bible study designed to help non-writers record their faith journey. She is a regular contributor to the Pearls of Promise blog and can be found on Twitter *@LisaGMick* or *lisamick@pearlsofpromiseministries.com.*

Lord of the Fork

Alma Jimenez Hall

I've struggled with losing weight all my life. I'd always said I wanted people to like me for who I am—not how much I weigh. Besides, there was so much pressure in my life, and eating was a break from it all.

My mom had become very ill, so I ate to combat the stress, and when she passed away, I ate for comfort... and became the heaviest I'd ever been.

The final straw came when my doctor told me my blood pressure was very high and if I couldn't bring it down, I'd need medication. I'd allowed food to control my life and wondered if I was going down the same path my mother had traveled with high blood pressure and diabetes.

Needing God's help, I searched His word for references to food. Surprisingly, I found scripture after scripture about food gluttony. I had no idea he had so much to say about food and our bodies. I discovered our Father cares a great deal about our health. We are body, soul, and spirit and He is concerned about the whole man or woman.

1 Corinthians 6:19-20 says: *Know ye not that your body is the temple of the Holy Ghost which is in you, which ye have of God, and ye are not your own? For ye are bought with a price: therefore glorify God in your body, and in your spirit, which are God's* (KJV).

So for me, losing weight meant getting in a group for accountability and support. With God's help, little by little, the weight came off. I lost over 50 lbs. I changed the way I shopped, cooked and ate. Do I still struggle at times? You bet. But with God, *I can do all things through Christ who strengthens me* (NKJV). Do I still, at times, let the fork become my Lord? Yes, but I have learned to be honest with myself and to get right back up when I fall. I simply forgive myself and get back to healthy eating.

I know that with every meal I can choose between health and gluttony. I know from experience how it feels to be unhappy and unhealthy because of gluttony and inactivity. So be encouraged! No matter where you find yourself today, you can be freed and be whole: body, soul, and spirit. I pray that you will let our Lord be the Lord of your fork and in the process become closer to Him and, *Taste and see that the LORD is good; blessed is the one who takes refuge in Him* (Psalm 34:8).

Alma Hall is a foodie, wellness/image coach, speaker and promoter. Contact her at *linkedin.com/in/almahall17* or *almahall9@gmail.com.*

Sudden Impact

Mary Ann Springer Moore

How can I impact my world for Christ TODAY? TODAY, I will start my day controlling my thoughts. I am a product of my thoughts; I want to be positive and encouraging. I will not be a victim of my circumstances. I will avoid gossip and negative attitudes. I will not let irritations take me to irrational thinking. May a positive attitude rule and reign.

TODAY, I will control my tongue. I will remember that God gave me two ears and one mouth. I will listen more than I speak. I will use my words to encourage others, not to correct them, or give them my opinion.

TODAY, I will be thankful for every minute and not waste my time worrying, gloating or embellishing self-pity. Time is a gift; that's why they call it the present. I will make time for loved ones, for that is the best way to say "I love you." I will spend my time helping others.

TODAY, I will focus on the right choices I have made. I will not focus on my past failures. We cannot change what we have done in the past, but we can, ask for forgiveness, and do the right thing. So, TODAY I will not go dumpster diving, digging up my weaknesses and failures. I will learn from my mistakes and use that to help others do the right thing.

TODAY, I will do the things I need to do. I will get organized and not procrastinate. I will focus on the talents I have. I will ask God for help in my weakness. For where I am weak, He is strong.

TODAY, *I can do everything through Him who gives me strength* (Philippians 4:13).

TODAY, I will surrender my right to be right. I will choose to be humble and look how I can serve, not be served.

TODAY, may I be used to bring the gospel of peace to all I encounter. May I understand that I am at the exact place and circumstance that God has placed me in for a reason and for a season. I may be the only Bible someone sees, and TODAY, may I remember people are watching me and respond the way God would have me respond.

TODAY, I will impact my world.

Mary Ann Springer Moore is a Christian motivational speaker in Northern California and is currently enrolled at Golden Gate Baptist Theological Seminary. She has led Bible study groups for 18 years, and mentored over 300 women. She also enjoys working with teens impacting the next generation spreading a "contagious Christian" lifestyle. Her life goal is to make a difference for Christ.

Stealing Home

Tina Hunt

It takes a lot of guts to steal home. The day I saw it on ESPN's SportsCenter, I stood in the living room, my mouth hanging open. It was an awesome play! My husband laughed at me because I kept repeating how amazing it was. The pitcher is closer to home plate than the runner at third base. He starts to run and the catcher hops up to let the pitcher know. The throw is close. The ump, in his animated fashion, signals the runner safe. The catcher is incensed. The runner trots off to the dugout like it was no big thing. I'm standing in my living room with my mouth agape.

I instantly saw the spiritual implications to this outstanding baseball feat. Stealing home takes absolute fearlessness. You have to run quick and hard. You have to be ready for a horrible crash with the catcher, which most likely will result in more than one bruise. Isn't this the type of determination that's required to live by faith? John writes that perfect love leaves no room for fear.

As I thought more about this I was reminded of Philippians 4:4-9. Paul says: *Always be full of joy in the Lord. I say it again—rejoice! Let everyone see that you are considerate in all you do. Remember, the Lord is coming soon. Don't worry about anything; instead, pray about everything.... And now, dear brothers and sisters, one final thing. Fix your thoughts on what is true, and honorable, and right, and pure, and lovely, and admirable. Think about things that are excellent and worthy of praise* (NLT).

I read those verses and I picture the runner with his

head down running full out for home, every move infused with intensity and determination. There is no hint of fear. There is no looking to the left or right. The runner receives the instruction from the coach and goes for it with his entire being. Can we do any less?

Well, of course we can...and we often do. The almost laughable thing is that we wonder why we are so easily thrown out of the game. Maybe it has something to do with the stubborn, independent streak that keeps us from being fully in the game and bringing our needs to our loving heavenly Father. Simply put, our choices have the potential to trip us up as we run the bases of life. We need to be wise in the way we choose to run.

I'm running flat-out and stealing home with both guts and glory. How about you?

Tina Hunt is a writer and speaker who you can find at *about.me/tina_hunt*. You can also follow her on Twitter *@tinamhunt*.

The Need for Naomis

Lisa Burkhardt Worley

Our ministry team had the opportunity to meet popular author and speaker, Liz Curtis Higgs recently. The creator of the "Bad Girls of the Bible" series has a book out called *The Girl's Still Got It* based on the book of Ruth.

Higgs has a contagious, exuberant personality and in many ways, she is like Ruth's mother-in-law, Naomi, a mentor, setting the example for us aspiring writers of how a successful author should act. Despite selling millions of books and speaking at over 1500 venues, there was no superstar bubble around her. Approachable and down-to-earth, she took photos with and autographed books for every woman who took the time to come see and meet her.

In our world today, women are starved for mentors. While men have the "good old boy" network down, it is my experience with women that there is too much competition and not enough connecting.

There is a great need for more Naomis!

In the book of Ruth, when Naomi decided to return to her homeland after losing her husband and sons, she instructed her newly widowed daughters-in-law, Orpah and Ruth, to return home to their parents because she couldn't offer them anything. Orpah moved on, but Ruth didn't abandon her mother-in-law, replying: *Don't urge me to leave you or to turn back from you. Where you go I will go, and where you stay, I will stay. Your people will be my people and your God my God* (Ruth 1:16).

Would anyone want to follow you?

I am currently facilitating a Bible study where every female in the study is younger than me. That might have been intimidating at one point in my life, but now God has brought me to a place where I embrace the responsibility of being a Naomi to these ladies. I want Christ to be so visible in me that they "want to go where I go" and desire "my God to be their God." I am praying to live a consistent life of faith, without hypocrisy, so that I am worthy of following.

It's a calling I am not able to answer on my own. Christ must do it through me.

So, what about you? Are you ready to take the leap to the next level, the elite class of Naomi nobility? If not, ask the Lord to infuse you with the passion to mentor, because there are countless women searching for their own personal Naomi. A perfect life is not required. A redeemed, imperfect life is the best teacher. As Jesus said in Matthew 9:37: *The harvest is plentiful but the workers are few.*

Lisa Burkhardt Worley is a former national television sports reporter, now Christian motivational speaker and writer and is the founder of Pearls of Promise Ministries, *pearlsofpromiseministries.com.* She is the co-author of the award winning manuscript, *If I Only Had...Following God's Path to Your Security* and is an editor for the *Pearls of Promise* devotional.

Traffic Jams and Leaky Faucets

Catherine Weiskopf

How do you feel about a traffic jam, a leaky faucet, a rainy day and friends moving away from you? I'm afraid to say I list events in two categories: those that make my life easier versus those that make my life harder. If I'm honest, my opinion really has nothing to do with what is best for another, or God's plans, but instead it's often about how it affects me.

A traffic jam makes ME late.

A leak in the faucet makes a mess for ME to clean up.

The rain causes ME to cancel our plans.

I realized this embarrassing concern for self when four friends announced moving plans. I didn't like how them moving would change my very comfortable, pleasant life. So what did I do about it? I tried to convince them to stay. Not out of concern for them; out of concern for, here's that word again, ME.

A friend who wanted a divorce needed to work harder on her marriage. Not because I thought it was against God's will, but because it would make my life and my children's lives less fun. To another friend who had upgrading on her mind, I tried to make a case for the "simple life." To a third, whose husband took a minister's job in another state, I wondered out loud if he was doing the right thing. To the fourth, moving so she'd be closer to her kids' school, I didn't think she should move to make her kids happy. Of course, she should stay here to make me happy.

We have an obsessively convenient easy life. That's what God wants for us, right? Isn't that what we often pray for? I know I did. Give me friends and fun and take all that unpleasantness far away from my galaxy. Whether I realize it or not, I often pray for an easy path.

But God's plans have nothing to do with play dates and socializing at the bus stop. In fact, God's plan has nothing to do with an easy life. Instead He promises us an "abundant life" in John 10:10: *The thief comes only to steal and kill and destroy. I came that they may have life and have it abundantly* (ESV).

So here's the choice. In one column is the easy life: free from pain and discomfort. In the next column is the abundant life, the rich life, filled with abundance and love. Which would I choose?

A traffic jam, a leaky faucet, rain, and even friends moving, maybe they don't belong on a list of things that make my life harder. Maybe they belong on an entirely different list: a list of things that make my life richly abundant.

Dear God, give me abundant life, and yes even if it's harder, messier, and more exhausting.

Catherine Weiskopf is the creative director of POP Ministries. She is a Christian and educational writer dedicated to helping others tell their stories. She is a regular contributor to the Pearls of Promise blog and can be found on Twitter *@Cweiskopf.*

More Than a Pie

Megan DiMaria

My Aunt Margaret created delightful pies with amazing flavors and textures. Strawberry-rhubarb pie, pecan pie, lemon meringue pie, mincemeat pie—I loved them all.

It was simple for Aunt Margaret to bake pies, and her results were always perfect. I spent many afternoons in her kitchen, standing side-by-side as the sun washed over her blue Delft-patterned wallpaper and illuminated the counter where she gave me pie lessons.

As a young wife and mother I bought all kinds of pie plates and pie cookbooks, desperately trying to duplicate the delicate flavor of Aunt Margaret's pies. Unfortunately, as my family can attest, the pie gene is absent from my DNA. My pie plates are rarely used, and all those pie cookbooks are gathering dust. But I look back on the days spent in that cozy kitchen and recall more than the measures of ingredients and the texture of crust. During those moments, Aunt Margaret taught me far more than how to combine flour and water and fruit and spices.

Her lessons taught me about the mighty power of gentle encouragement. During the mixing and measuring, Aunt Margaret made me believe I could become a world-class pastry chef or a lawyer or journalist or whatever I chose. Through the simple act of baking pies together, my heart was awakened to possibilities, and my confidence was strengthened. All because she gave me the small, simple gift of pie lessons and the powerful words, "You can do it."

Do not despise these small beginnings, for the Lord rejoices to see the work begin, to see the plumb line in Zerubbabel's hand (Zechariah 4:10, NLT).

Megan DiMaria is an author and speaker who encourages women to embrace life's demands and delights. She is the author of two women's fiction novels, *Searching for Spice* and *Out of Her Hands*. Her website is *megandimaria.com*. Befriend her at *Facebook.com/megandimaria*.

Pearls of
Faith

God and Elvis: A Big Fish Story

Catherine Weiskopf

*I*n them is fulfilled the prophecy of Isaiah: You will be ever hearing but never understanding; you will be ever seeing but never perceiving *(Matthew 13:14).*

Hearing God's voice is like seeing Elvis. I should know; I saw Elvis on a recent trip to Hawaii. We were staying in a resort on the big island where a barracuda named Elvis lived. He traveled the salty canal waters, making appearances at various locations, but you had to watch carefully to get a glimpse. Elvis was large, but quick. I thought I caught a flash of silver out of the corner of my eye, but I couldn't be sure it was him. I wanted a good look; I waited by the canal and watched because I was determined to see the famous fish. Then I saw a small wave moving out over the otherwise still, dark blue, shallow water. It was coming towards me. I waited. The ripple came closer and closer and, ah! The barracuda! A ripple on top of the water meant a barracuda underneath. Now I knew what to look for. Now I could spot Elvis easily.

When I saw Elvis that day, I had been praying for more awareness of God's voice. I realized instantly that seeing Elvis was like hearing God. I first of all had to want to see Elvis. To hear God I had to begin my journey with a prayer of intent.

Next, I had to stop and patiently watch the canal to catch a view of Elvis. When I had trouble seeing Elvis I could have run up and down the stream frantically looking for him. This is sometimes how we try to hear God, especially when we have a problem that "needs" an immediate solution. But having patience means spending time in silence, it means not scheming to fix things, and it means not working things out my way. I had to start giving myself quiet time so God could be heard and then real fixes could happen.

Finally, to see Elvis, I had to become in tune with the signs of a big fish moving under the water—the ripples on top. In terms of listening to God, I had to learn to hear His gentle voice. Elijah (1 Kings 19:9-13) looked for God in big things: an earthquake, a fire, and a storm, but he did not find Him until he listened to a gentle whisper. That is God's way. He speaks to us through coincidence, gentle tugs on our hearts, and whispers.

It is true that many people never recognize God's gentle voice in the midst of their busy lives. It is also true that many people who stayed at our hotel never saw Elvis.

Dear God, I know that you're speaking, but often I don't hear. Open my ears, God. Make me aware of your gentle voice. Give me the intent, patience and attention to hear your voice.

Catherine Weiskopf is the creative director of Pearls of Promise Ministries. She is the author of three educational books for children. She most recently co-authored the award winning manuscript, *If I Only Had... Following God's Path to Your Security*. Email her at *cweiskopf@pearlsofpromiseministries.com*.

The Apartment

Rebecca Carrell

F or our light and momentary troubles are achieving for us an eternal glory that far outweighs them all (2 Corinthians 4:17).

My sister and her family relocated over the summer, and did some major renovations before they moved in. Because they sold their house sooner than anticipated, Liz, her three young children, husband, and two large golden retrievers crammed themselves into a 900 square foot apartment.

When I went to visit, Liz warned me that it was cramped. "And I haven't done a thing to it," she added, while leading the kids and me through the front door.

She was right. Stark white walls boasted no room-warming pictures. Only the bare-essentials when it came to furniture. No curtains on the windows, no rugs on the floors. It was very clear that this was not where Liz was focusing her attention.

"I bet you're ready to get out of here," I said to Liz, smiling.

"I am," she replied, "but I've been so busy working on the new house that I don't even really see it." I nodded in agreement. I know what it's like to be so wrapped up in something that your current circumstances fade into the background. Plus, there's no sense putting too much time and energy into the temporary, when you could be investing in the permanent.

Do not store up for yourselves treasures on earth, where moths and vermin destroy, and where thieves break in and steal. But store up for yourselves treasures in heaven, where moths and vermin do not destroy, and where thieves do not break in and steal. For where your treasure is, there your heart will be also (Matthew 6:19-21).

Imagine the peace and freedom we could enjoy if we would only remember that our current circumstances are merely temporary housing when contrasted with eternity. Don't be concerned with what goes on the walls. Don't worry too much about rugs on the floors. Don't be preoccupied with gadgets and knickknacks and things.

What keeps you awake at night? No matter how big it looks right now, it is temporary. What steals your attention away from heavenly things? Your Heavenly Father is jealous for your every thought. He gave you this life; He wants you to enjoy it, to know the richness of the abundant life lived in Christ. Let your mind wander to the things of Christ. Dwell in His Word. Linger in His Presence. Breathe in His Spirit. Live out His love. He wants you to know that, compared to the glory awaiting you, *this life* is a 900 square foot apartment.

Rebecca Ashbrook Carrell has been a radio personality in the Dallas Ft. Worth area since 1998. She left full-time radio to found LSS Ministries but can still be heard on a part-time basis at Christian talk station 90.9 KCBI. Rebecca writes and teaches Bible studies and authors a devotional on her website, *LoveServeShine.com.*

Faith Does Set Us Free

Beth Shriver

*B*ut our citizenship is in heaven, and from it we await a Savior, the Lord Jesus Christ, who will transform our lowly body to be like His glorious body, by the power that enables Him even to subject all things to Himself (Philippians 3:20-21, ESV).

Although Marlin Yoder didn't grow up in the Amish community, his grandfather did, and all of the relatives before him. His last name speaks of his Amish roots. When I first started writing Amish, he told me if I ever needed information, he had lots of stories. And he was a great storyteller! I knew he was sick, and I planned to visit him. I also wanted to find out why his father left the Amish community. But he passed away two weeks later. I missed out on saying goodbye to one of the most admirable people I know, and hearing firsthand about the true-life experiences of the characters I craft every day. Marlin would have made them real.

His Amish relatives drove from Kansas to the funeral. They were an Old Order group who wore the traditional black and white clothing. It was interesting to hear them reminisce about Marlin, and even more so what they chose to remember him by; it was *so* Amish. He had a birdcall no one could quite figure out. He had an incredible work ethic that is so common for the Amish, and he loved to sing! Amish sing for two, sometimes three, hours straight at services. Can you imagine? My throat's dry already! And he clapped his hands, which isn't so uncommon for any of us, but not for hours like he did. He loved his students unconditionally, and prayed without ceasing. We've all heard comments like that, but Marlin truly lived that way.

What would my friends and family say about me? Probably not about birdcalls, singing, and clapping. Maybe the work ethic part, and I do pray, but not compared to Marlin. Would something profound or really deep come to mind? I hope so, but probably not like the comments I heard about Marlin.

This experience has made me think about how people will see me when it's my time to go. I'm learning how to make my life simpler, yet memorable, and perhaps little things like birdcalls and singing your heart out are more important than I thought.

Faith Step: Seize the moment each day. If you could write your obituary what would it say?

Beth Shriver is the author of *Annie's Truth, Grace Given* and *Healing Grace*. You can find her at *BethShriverWriter.com*.

Faith and Shavu'ot

Janna Longfellow Hughes

For those whom He foreknew He also predestined to be conformed to the image of His Son, in order that He might be the firstborn within a large family (Romans 8:29, NRSV).

The creamy, sweet taste of cheesecake filled my mouth. We stood in the kitchen annex of a Messianic Synagogue following their holiday celebration. I listened to the friendly woman nearby explain, "We celebrate the Feast of Shavu'ot seven weeks after Passover by eating milk products. It reminds us of the milk of God's Word that nurtures us. Many bring a First Fruit Offering."

My heart gently warmed as we spoke of Jesus the Word made flesh who became our first fruits—the first born of a large family. Two millennia ago, our Passover lamb gave His life's blood on a cruel execution stake.

Why did God require the sacrifice of His only Son? It was the only way. Not one of us could be the spotless lamb. God's overwhelming love moved Him to supply the lamb without blemish on our behalf. He paid the terrible price we could not pay.

Again, I savored the delicious celebratory cheese cake. I thought about the sweet savor to the Heavenly Father that Jesus must have been when He willingly became the Way for us. Jesus became the open door to God. Now we can choose to become part of God's family. Through His life in us, we too can be a sweet taste to the Heavenly Father as the image of Christ is formed in us.

Father, help us to be transformed into the lovely image of Jesus day by day, Amen.

Janna Longfellow Hughes is a television producer and published writer who can be found at *JannaLongfellowHughes.com*. Janna has also written an ebook, *DEVELOP YOUR STORY - Tools for Building a Bridge to Your Audience* (download free at Janna's website).

Leap of Faith

Catherine Weiskopf

Do not fear what they fear; do not be frightened (1 Peter 3:14).

My 9-year-old son's cry of pain interrupted a nice meal with family. He clutched his throat as he whispered, "bone." The tiny perch inflicted revenge with its sharp but minuscule bone.

"Eat something and the bone will go down," I said, handing my son a piece of bread. Agitated and still holding his throat, he shoved the bread away and grabbed a piece of paper. He scrawled down question after question:

Is it bleeding?

What if it doesn't go down?

Will I be able to breathe?

I patiently answered each question as the drool dripped off his chin. I hated to see him in pain when it wasn't necessary. "Don't write anymore questions," I said. "Just do it." I knew what would happen when he swallowed the bread.

"Remember Indiana Jones and his leap of faith," I explained, talking about the movie, *Indiana Jones and the Last Crusade*. "He couldn't see the pathway. All he saw was a cliff, but he still stepped out into thin air over a deep chasm. This is your leap of faith. You don't know for sure what's going to happen. I've had a lot of experience with bones in my throat. Swallowing bread has always helped. Do you trust what I say?" I asked.

He wasn't sure.

"This is your Indiana Jones moment. You can either swallow the bread and see what happens or not swallow the bread and have the fish bone stay in your throat."

I wish I could say he immediately took the bread, swallowed it and everything was fine, but he was a reluctant hero. The throat clutching and tears went on for another hour. More drool, more questions, more pain, but then finally, a leap. He ate the bread and instantly the bone went down. His pain seemed so silly to me until I realized we have a lot in common.

Like my son, I often stand on the edge of a decision-cliff filled with terror: should I speak at the conference, should I write a middle-grade book, should I fly to China? I often put one foot out over the chasm and pull it back. "Just a few more questions, God:

Is it going to be painful?

Are you sure I can do this?

Will I fall flat on my face?"

Just like I assured my son, God assures me, "It'll be ok, but you have to leap." I know my choice is to either live, metaphorically, with a fish bone in my throat or take a leap of faith and have freedom.

Dear God, just like my son was terrified of the pain of a fish bone, I am often scared to be brave and step out with you into the unknown. Forgive me for my lack of faith and help me to be willing to follow you out over the edge of the cliff of my comfort zone.

Catherine Weiskopf is the creative director of Pearls of Promise Ministries. She is the author of three educational books for children. She most recently co-authored the award winning manuscript *If I Only Had... Following God's Path to Your Security.* Email her at *cweiskopf@pearlsofpromiseministries.com.*

Mind Markers

Lisa Burkhardt Worley

One day in Bible study, we were asked to reflect on our spiritual walk and how far we had come. It is important to remember the times when God seemed especially close and to also recall the difficult times God has brought us through. This can help us during spiritually dry periods when we need encouragement.

In Old Testament times, when God made His presence known to leaders of the faith, they would often build an altar at that spot. After God revealed Himself to Jacob in Genesis 35, Jacob constructed an altar and named the place where the altar sat, "El Bethel" which means "God of Bethel." In Joshua 5, Joshua asked the twelve leaders of the tribes to set up twelve stones to serve as a reminder of when God stopped the flow of the Jordan River so the Ark of the Covenant could pass through. After 40 days and nights of rain, when Noah, his family, and all the animals emerged from the ark, the first thing Noah did was build an altar to offer sacrifices to the Lord. God had brought them through the storm.

God brings us through many storms in our own lives, and when we emerge, we don't have to build an altar, but we can consciously create a "mind marker" to forever remember God's grace. I can remember my faith being tested when our youngest son had problems at birth and ended up in neo-natal intensive care for nine days. Through our prayers and the prayers of the church, we were carried by God through this time. Our second born is now a healthy sixteen year old boy! I will never forget that stretch of time and think back on it when our son tries our patience!

We can also go back to our "mind markers" in our spiritual journey. One of my markers is when my friend introduced me to Christ in my high school freshman English class. God worked through my friend to change my life forever. I have another "mind marker" when I rededicated my life to Christ in 1993 as well as "mind markers" for all the times God spoke directly to me about something I needed to do in my life. I don't receive direct revelation from God often, so when I do it is special, life changing, and worthy of a "mind marker." On those days when God seems far away and I am not feeling spiritual, I remember all the times God was so close I could touch Him, and it boosts my spiritual low.

Psalm 77:11-12 says, *I will remember the deeds of the Lord; yes, I will remember your miracles of long ago. I will meditate on all your works and consider all your mighty deeds*. What mighty deeds and miracles has God done in your life? If you haven't already done it, create some "mind markers" today so you will never forget the works of the Lord in your own life.

Lisa Burkhardt Worley is a Christian motivational speaker and writer and is the founder of Pearls of Promise Ministries, *pearlsofpromiseministries.com*. She is the co-author of the award winning manuscript, *If I Only Had...Following God's Path to Your Security*, and is an editor for the *Pearls of Promise* devotional.

Spiritual Defroster

Catherine Weiskopf

We don't yet see things clearly. We're squinting in a fog, peering through a mist. But it won't be long before the weather clears and the sun shines bright! We'll see it all then, see it all as clearly as God sees us, knowing Him directly just as He knows us! (1 Corinthians 13:12, MSG)

Eight a.m. on a cool fall day my daughter and I headed out to her soccer game. Starting the car, frosty windows surrounded us. From inside the car I saw the world through a translucent haze. I turned on the defroster and waited. Air burst out, and an inch near the base of the window became clear. If I bent over, and strained my neck I could see clearly. Slowly the clearness inched its way up the foggy window, unclouded glass taking over haze. After a few minutes of patience my window was good to go.

Driving off immediately and not waiting patiently for the windows to clear would have been dangerous. My immediate thought was to connect the frosted window to my foggy spiritual vision. Often I wake up in full speed not even checking in with God before I jump into the day's tasks. I race from place to place, task to task, without seeing my world and the people around me clearly through God's eyes. When I can't see where I am going spiritually, I can and do drive off His road. When a friend slights me, when I see something I want but can't have, or someone insults one of my children, my wheel jerks to the left and soon I am on another path driving down a gravel road where I'm likely to slide into the ditch. Minute by minute I need to use my spiritual defrosters: the

Bible, religious books, church, praying, and listening to God, so I can find my way back onto God's road.

That morning, I would never have driven without defrosting my window, yet many days I start my day without turning on my spiritual defroster. While driving with foggy windows is dangerous, living with unclear spiritual vision has even more devastating consequences.

Dear God, help me to be more aware of when my spiritual vision is getting cloudy and I need your defrosting to see clearly. Help me to take the time to spend time with you so that I can see your spiritual road distinctly.

Catherine Weiskopf is the creative director of Pearls of Promise Ministries. She is the author of three educational books for children. She most recently co-authored the award winning manuscript *If I Only Had... Following God's Path to Your Security.* Email her at *cweiskopf@pearlsof-promiseministries.com.*

The Ring

Sally Metzger

I *will not forget you! See, I have engraved you on the palms of my hands* (Isaiah 49:15-16).

"Are we almost there?" whined four-year-old Brian thirty minutes into our twelve-hour drive. Our vacation at the beach had been carefully planned. We were a family with great expectations!

"Brian, honey, maybe you could entertain your brother," I said, looking back at one-year-old Jeremy, whose face was contorted, ready to burst into tears of boredom.

Brian reached up and shielded his ears. The silence in the car had been only a brief intermission—a gift of Jeremy's ten-minute nap.

The trailer we had borrowed swayed from side to side in the strong wind, and the bike rack on top of our car caught the wind and produced a mournful howl. The crying baby, whining child, and howling bike rack made quite a trio, serenading my husband and me as we drove down the lonesome highway.

Our nights were slightly more difficult than our days. At 2:00 a.m. on the first night, I stood outside our thin-walled trailer to check the noise level of Jeremy's shrill cries. Just as I'd feared, our son was letting everyone in the park know he was not a happy camper.

We enjoyed the beach until Jeremy discovered he liked the taste of sand. He thought having his mouth emptied was a wonderful game and added variety by changing the direction and speed of his crawl from the blanket.

Then, to top it all off, there was my ring. On the fifth night, I sat beside a crackling campfire, staring at the empty prongs that should have held the diamond of my engagement ring. I searched our trailer thoroughly. I memorized the indentations the furniture made in the carpet's worn nap. The diamond was nowhere to be found.

Even eternal vacations come to an end. As we pulled the camper into our driveway, I thought I'd grasped the gift of the trip. I was grateful that I had a home to return to and happy to help my husband carry two sleeping little boys into their waiting beds. Life was about being thankful—in spite of what happens.

The next morning I swept the trailer one last time so the camper could be returned. I scooped up a bookmark I'd bought on the trip: It read, *See, I will not forget you. I have carved you on the palms of my hands.* I glanced back at the floor where I'd retrieved the bookmark. Glistening in the light that streamed from the tiny skylight above me lay my diamond.

Surely there aren't always happy endings. We can't demand them as proof that we are safe in His hands. Only *faith* can promise that. But there are those little reassurances. We must carve them into our hearts for safekeeping. We may need to draw on them for the true challenges of life. Our God is the same, yesterday, today, and tomorrow. God is good. All the time.

Sally Metzger, M.T.S., is a Dallas speaker and spiritual director who seeks to help others deepen intimacy with God. Sally taught theology at Jesuit College Preparatory School of Dallas for 21 years and is currently writing a book on Ignatian Spirituality. Visit *sallymetzgerauthor.com* or email *smetzgerauthor@live.com.*

Two Inches

Lisa Burkhardt Worley

My husband and I love to play golf, and play together almost every week. I have been a golf nut all my life. A couple of years ago, however, golf gave me more than a fun day with my husband; it gave me a critical reminder about the brevity of life.

My husband and I were over halfway through the round at our local course when a father and his son asked if they could "play through." My husband said to wave them on so I moved my golf cart over to the cart path and motioned for them to go ahead and play. I first watched the man's son drive so I'd know where the ball was going, then decided to take off in the cart to get further out, so I would not be in danger of getting hit by the father's tee shot.

I had only traveled a few feet when I heard a loud CRACK. I was stunned initially, but quickly realized that a golf ball had connected with my head. The sound off my forehead was so loud that the father hitting the ball from the tee thought his shot hit the cart instead. (In his defense, he thought I had moved out of the way already and didn't see me when he hit his tee shot.)

I shouted to my husband on the other side of the fairway, who also heard the loud CRACK, "Hurry over here, I've been hit!" The knot on my head swelled out into a very unattractive ball and upon realizing how close the shot came to my temple, I began to cry. Fortunately, the CT Scan did not show a fracture in my skull or any internal bleeding, but the doctor reconfirmed that if the ball had found my temple, only two inches away, it would have been a different story. Two inches was the difference between life and death!

This experience was a reminder that each day of life we receive is a gift from God. We need to make the most of it for we do not know when we will be called to our heavenly home. I have had three near-death experiences like this, perhaps as a reminder that I need to stay the course in my faith journey. Psalm 90:12 reminds us, *Teach us to number our days, that we may gain a heart of wisdom.*

If our life ended today, would we have regrets about our faithfulness or would we be able to confidently walk through the pearly gates, knowing we had given it our all? We must learn to number our days and make every day count for eternity.

Lisa Burkhardt Worley is a Christian motivational speaker and writer and is the founder of Pearls of Promise Ministries, *pearlsofpromiseministries.com.* She is the co-author of the award winning manuscript, *If I Only Had...Following God's Path to Your Security* and is co-authoring a Bible study about how God takes us out of the world to do the unpopular.

Why God?

Rebecca Carrell

These have come so that the proven genuineness of your faith—of greater worth than gold, which perishes even though refined by fire—may result in praise, glory and honor when Jesus Christ is revealed (1 Peter 1:7).

I can clearly remember the day I joined the track team. Our coach, Mr. Liese, made each of us run a timed mile. At the start of the season, a good time would be six minutes. A great time would be five-and-a-half. I ran it in a shade over eight minutes and I thought I was dying.

On more than one occasion, I recall Mr. Liese really laying into me. He never went easy on me, even though there were many, many other runners far more worthy of his attention and efforts.

As we moved into the final quarter of the year, he encouraged me to sign up for his strength and conditioning class, promising the workouts would improve my running. "What does he care," I wondered, "I'm getting ready to graduate." Nevertheless, I took the class.

I came to respect the executor of my torture, realizing that the old me had to be broken down if the new me were to emerge. I started to push myself harder. If he said, "Run five miles this weekend," I ran seven. I altered my diet and streamlined my lifestyle, and at the regional track meet, the state meet qualifier, I saw the fruit of my efforts.

I ran the fastest mile of my life. It took every ounce of strength I had. I did not qualify for the state meet, but I accomplished far more than I'd ever dreamed possible, all because of a coach who would not give up on an overweight, insecure, rookie senior.

At the team banquet, I watched as the awards were given out. I beamed, heart bursting, as my sister and her relay team received recognition. And although I knew my name would not be called, I had never felt so full.

"And most improved goes to...Rebecca Ashbrook!"

A lump formed in my throat as I arose to accept the award. Beaming, Mr. Liese handed me the medal and pulled me in for a hug. "I never let up on you, kiddo," he whispered, "because I knew you had it in you. I knew it!"

What a beautiful thing, to know that someone sees *more* when they look at you.

What does God see when He looks at you?

Just as my track coach pushed me and worked me until I could barely stand it, God will work you and push you until you fulfill the glorious purpose He has called you to. He will chip away at your pride and sand down your rough edges. He will put people in your path to irritate you, exposing character traits *within you* that need to go, so that you can become a reflection of Jesus. He loves you too much *not* to, my friend, because when God looks at you He sees *more!*

Rebecca Ashbrook Carrell has been a radio personality in the Dallas Ft. Worth area since 1998. She left full-time radio to found LSS Ministries but can still be heard on a part-time basis at Christian talk station 90.9 KCBI. Rebecca writes and teaches Bible studies and authors a devotional on her website, *LoveServeShine.com.*

Pearls of Comfort

A Happy Ending

Lisa Burkhardt Worley

My all-time favorite movies are classics like *Sleepless in Seattle* and *When Harry Met Sally*. I remember the first time I ever watched *Frosty the Snowman*. I cried when old Frosty melted because I didn't know the rest of the story. When Frosty came back to life, let's just say I was satisfied. I'm a romanticist and love a happy ending!

However, during our lifetime, not everything ends happily. Trials occur, sickness weakens and relationships sever. God never promised our lives would be easy. In fact it says plainly in John 16:33 that *in this world you will have trouble.*

My most difficult days were also the stretches of time where I found myself feverishly pursuing God's presence. I wanted to know He was near. What about you?

While we may experience trouble in this world, there is hope. God writes a happy ending for anyone who believes in His son, Jesus Christ.

For the Lord Himself will come down from heaven, with a loud command, with the voice of the archangel and with the trumpet call of God, and the dead in Christ will rise first. After that, we who are still alive and are left will be caught up together with them in the clouds to meet the Lord in the air. And so we will be with the Lord forever (1 Thessalonians 4:16-17).

An unhappy end in this world is not the end of a believer's story! Eternal life with God is written on the final page. That is worth celebrating!

No matter what you may be experiencing now, remember that God loves you so much that He has provided a happy ending for your life. Isn't it nice to know the rest of the story?

Lisa Burkhardt Worley is a former national television sports reporter who is now a Christian motivational speaker and writer with Pearls of Promise Ministries, *pearlsofpromiseministries.com.* She is the co-author of the award winning manuscript, *If I Only Had...Following God's Path to Your Security,* and co-editor of the *Pearls of Promise* devotional.

Breathing New Life

Jennifer Mersberger

I have a brown thumb. A few summers ago a local home improvement store held a huge sale on trees. The trees were young and small but already hardy and green.

I managed to kill mine even though it was a notoriously low maintenance tree with instructions to simply plant it and watch it grow. I brought it home and within a week all its leaves were gone. Several neighbors took advantage of the same sale at the same store. Their trees flourished throughout the season.

Why did their saplings survive and mine didn't? Was it the tree? The soil? Did I water too much? Not enough? I had tons of questions and not many answers. Feeling defeated, I dug up my tree, put it back in its bucket and stuck it in a corner of my yard until I had time to take it to the trash.

The next spring while doing yard work, I noticed the abandoned tree. My heart sank a little as I remembered my dream for the shade it would produce. Sighing, I decided now was as good a time as any to take it to the trash. As I bent down to pick up the bucket, I saw them...little green leaves. Upon further inspection, the branches were full of little leaves popping their way out of the dormant bark. It was alive! I ran to tell my husband and clear my tree-killing name.

Much too often we treat our dreams or aspirations

just like I treated that tree. We embrace the possibilities they may offer, but become discouraged when things don't grow as planned. After searching for answers and comparing our results with those of other people, we become defeated and give up. Sometimes we give up for good. We drag our "trees" to the curb to be tossed out forever, never giving them a second chance. Other times we ignore our hopes and dreams, keeping them tucked into a corner wishing they would become something more.

God has a purpose for your hopes and dreams. You may obtain your actual dream. Or maybe those dreams lead you to where God wants you to go. Either way, they can be used for His glory but not if you throw them away.

Do you have dormant trees in your life? Are you still looking for signs of life or have you given up on them? I only wanted a little shade; now I have eight trees, alive and growing more each day. Give God your dreams; He just may breathe new life into them.

For I know the plans I have for you, declares the Lord, plans to prosper you and not to harm you, plans to give you hope and a future (Jeremiah 29:11).

Jennifer Mersberger is an Amazon Top 15 Christian author, public speaker, and founder of Lamplight Ministry. Through her Bible studies and weekly blog, Jennifer uses her unique perspective and fun sense of humor to help you see God in your everyday. Get to know her at *lamplightministry.com and Facebook.com/JenniferMersberger.*

Are We Being Watched?

Lisa Burkhardt Worley

One day, while spending time with family, we discussed heaven and the possibility that our deceased loved ones were watching our lives from above. Neither my husband nor I have parents left. My husband's dad, who passed on a couple of years ago, was the last remaining parent/grandparent left in our small family. My sister-in-law, Sue, who has a kitchen table at her lake house that belonged to her deceased mom and dad, joked that her dad would be unhappy if he saw my water glass on the table without a coaster!

All kidding aside, there is scriptural evidence our lives are on display. Hebrews 12:1-2 affirms this thought: *Therefore, since we are surrounded by such a great cloud of witnesses, let us throw off everything that hinders and the sin that so easily entangles. And let us run with perseverance the race marked out for us, fixing our eyes on Jesus, the pioneer and perfecter of faith. For the joy set before Him He endured the cross, scorning its shame, and sat down at the right hand of the throne of God.*

I want to believe that my parents, grandparents, and ancestors before that are in that great crowd of witnesses cheering me on to do the right thing in my faith journey!

One of the ancestors I never met was my great-great grandfather, Abram Weaver. Abram Weaver was an itinerant pastor who began his life in Salisbury, North Carolina, but his ministry travel eventually brought him to Georgetown, Texas. I came across his three page autobiography a few years ago, and after reading it realized my goal would be to have the kind of great faith Abram Weaver had. He summarized his life in the last paragraph of his writing: "I was engaged in the active work of the ministry just fifty years. During that time, I preached more than three thousand sermons to more than three hundred thousand people. I superintended the building of three, up-to-date, new churches and married a great many, smoothed the dying pillow of hundreds, who I shall see again, 'Beyond the sunset's purple rim.' I lament my inefficiency, repent my mistakes, love my Redeemer and hope to find rest in Heaven."

I believe Abram Weaver is in that great cloud of witnesses along with all of those relatives who have professed their faith in Jesus Christ and who have gone before me. My great-great grandfather's amazing testimony encourages me to persevere, as I attempt to do the work the Lord has set before me. What about you? Who is watching you right now as you make your journey through life?

Lisa Burkhardt Worley is a former national sports reporter and founder of Pearls of Promise Ministries. You can find her at *pearlsofpromiseministries.com*. Lisa is also the co-author of the award winning manuscript, *If I Only Had...Following God's Path to Your Security.*

Casting Cares

Stacy Voss

I recall the many hours spent at the lake growing up, hoping to catch dinner but knowing it rarely happened. My dad would untangle our fishing lines, fix the proper weights and bobbers and hand us the poles. Our girliness would disappear as he gave us the worms. What normally would be gross became fun as we played with them before twisting and tying them onto the hook. Then we'd cast out our lines. We'd watch in anticipation for a few minutes, but before long, the sight of the non-moving bobber bored us. Propping our poles on a rock, we'd run off to play. A few hours later, we'd reel in the line, only to discover an empty hook, reminding us that the very thing we'd been hoping for was closer than we realized.

Jesus understands fishing better than this novice. But He still lets me fish the same way I did as a child. I might finger my worries for a short period, but then I'll meticulously fasten them to the line. Maybe I'll even poke my finger a time or two. But once they're on, I'm invited to simply cast them out, giving them over to the Lord.

Psalm 55:22 says, *Cast your cares on the LORD and He will sustain you; He will never let the righteous be shaken.* Based on this truth, casting the line out is all that is required of me. Then I get to run off and play or go about the everyday duties life requires of me. I can do whatever I want, but I don't need to keep fingering my worry "bait." I just get to cast it out. Then, when I reel in my line at the end of the day, my "bait" and my worries will be gone. And that's no fisherman's tale.

Dear God, thank you that I can give you all my fears and anxieties. Amen.

Stacy Voss is the founder of Eyes of Your Heart Ministries (*eyesofyourheart. com*). She is known for her ability to bring biblical characters and principles to life in thought-provoking, transformative ways. She lives in Colorado with her husband and their two energetic kids.

The Gift of Comfort

Janna Longfellow Hughes

Eureka! I found a floral gift more stunning than a gemstone. The tall, ceramic white pot held two towering orchids. Below their milky blooms that arched downward a red bromeliad and a yellow one stretched up toward them.

I rubbed the rigid bromeliad leaves and recognized that despite their beauty, this gift was temporal. It could not compare to the eternal gifts that come from above.

Jesus promised us a Gift of Comfort. He said, *the Comforter, which is the Holy Ghost, whom the Father will send in my name, He shall teach you all things, and bring all things to your remembrance, whatsoever I have said unto you* (John 14:15, KJV).

His gift came on the Day of Pentecost (Acts 2:1-4). It came like the sound of a blowing, violent wind from heaven that filled the house where Jesus' followers met. They saw what looked like tongues of fire. All of them were filled with the Holy Spirit and they spoke in other languages as the Spirit enabled them.

On that historic day, Jerusalem spilled over with people who were there to celebrate the Feast of Shavuot. A crowd of those travelers gathered around Jesus' followers wondering how these Jews spoke in the native tongues of many visitors present. Peter seized that opportunity to address the gathering crowd. *Repent and be baptized, every one of you, in the name of Jesus Christ for the forgiveness of your sins, he said. And you will receive the gift of the Holy Spirit* (Acts 2:38).

About 3,000 accepted his message, were baptized, and received his gift.

Every good and perfect gift is from above, coming down from the Father of the heavenly lights, who does not change like shifting shadows (James 1:17).

God's gift is eternal. My perfect gift died. His amazing gift lives. We can accept Peter's message of the gift of God's Holy Spirit. We may receive comfort from this gift by remembering Jesus' words.

Dear Heavenly Father, help us to receive your gift of the Comforter and help us to recognize your Pearls of Comfort — every word Jesus said to us.

Janna Longfellow Hughes is a writer and television producer who has written ebook, *Develop Your Story - Tools for Building a Bridge to Your Audience* (download free at *JannaLongfellowHughes.com*, a gift to you). Find her at *JannaLongfellowHughes.com* blog and Vimeo channel, *vimeo.com/jannahughes.*

Emmanuel: God With Us

Tina Hunt

God...creator, sustainer, Holiness, worthy of worship and praise.

God...all knowing, always present, sovereign.

God...grace, love, glorious and amazing.

God...father, mother, friend, forgiver, redeemer, restorer.

God WITH us.

God...the one who is beyond time, who knows all, squeezed into NOW. He climbed into time.

He is with us: knowing hurt of loss of father; disrespect and discrediting of family (remember, his brothers thought he was crazy). He knew hunger, thirst, and exhaustion. He knew pain, dying the most painful and humiliating of deaths. He knew the loss of a friend. He knew what it was like to be lied about. He knew what it was like to be misunderstood. He knew anger and disappointment.

He had diaper rash, zits, hangnails, smashed thumbs.

He knew how to party and how to pray.

He knew the glory of heaven, but drew near and crawled into our existence.

God with US.

You, with all the stuff that frustrates, irritates, and separates me from you.

Me, well, I guess the same could be said about me from your perspective.

So He chose us, individually and corporately. Which was more important to Him? I'm not sure. His coming was for young and old, educated and farmhands, men and women. His coming was announced to those who were looking, and dropped as a bombshell on some guys hanging out in the fields.

Maybe I would do better to not ask the question. Or, to ask a different one. Maybe if I could get a grip on the fact that His name is God with us and not God with me, I would realize in a whole new way how much He loves you, what incredible value you hold to Him. And beyond just looking at you differently, perhaps I could look at "us" differently. Perhaps I wouldn't be so quick to draw lines of differentiation and separation. If I could wrap my brain around how loved and treasured we all are by God and I really began to live that way, then...then maybe there would be fewer bombs, less hate, less ugliness.

That's why these words and why this name is so special to me. In Christmas, like no other time, I celebrate hope—hope that came in the form of a baby. Hope that holds within the form of one so small; a hugeness that defies everything I see and touch, and feel and calls me to look at it fresh and new...and with you.

Tina Hunt is a writer and speaker who you can find at *about.me/tina_ hunt*. You can also follow her on Twitter *@tinamhunt*.

God Keeps His Promises

Kristi Melvin

My children have been the start of many great conversations between God and me. Can anyone relate?

It was a typical morning at our house. We went through the usual routine and then ventured out of the house for a few hours. I was driving and remember being just beyond our neighborhood when I noticed the gray clouds moving in our direction. Our oldest son, Kaleb, who was around three years old, managed to put together a sentence I'll never forget, "Mom, a rainbow's coming." I was immediately struck by his comment. It caused my mind and heart to move. My thoughts were something along the lines of, "Lord, how often do I worry about the storms of life and forget to rest in your promises?"

I recall that day often. Just when it's needed, God uses this sweet occurrence to remind me that a rainbow is coming. He makes all things beautiful in His time. In Psalm 145:13-14 He assures us, *The LORD is faithful to all His promises and loving toward all He has made. The LORD upholds all those who fall and lifts up all who are bowed down.*

In Genesis 9, God made a promise to Noah that the earth would never be flooded again, and the rainbow in the sky would be a sign of this promise. Today we still see the same beautiful reminder that Noah saw.

Rainbows still appear. Isn't it marvelous to spot a rainbow in the sky? I never grow tired of seeing them.

Are you in the midst of an impossible struggle? The storms of life may be looming, and they are certain to come and go. It's good to know that there's a rainbow coming.

Kristi Melvin works part time as a church office secretary. She is passionate about supporting her husband, Kris, who is a minister to youth and her 2 sons, Kaleb and Keaton who are the lights of their lives.

Remember the Redbird

Lisa Burkhardt Worley

I took all the ornaments off our Christmas tree yesterday. I find it somewhat sad, because the Christmas tree and the season of Christmas is a time of year that I enjoy a great deal. However, I did discover I take more time to examine my ornaments when taking them down versus putting them up. I am in such a hurry to get the tree decorated, that it's more about getting it done, than about sentimentality.

As I laid the ornaments on my dining room table, preparing them to be wrapped and stored, memories came flooding back. There was the "My First Kissmas" ornament, given to my husband and me from my mother-in-law, Sally, after we first got married. There was the stork ornament I was given by my husband when I was pregnant with our first child. Other ornaments reminded me of places we lived or visited over the years. The many crosses I put on the tree represent why we celebrate Christmas in the first place.

I also noticed we have more redbird ornaments than I realized. While I was Christmas shopping this year, it seems the redbird was predominant everywhere: on candles, Christmas plates, and ornaments. It was as if God was telling me to make note of the redbird.

The redbird carries great significance for a young friend of mine, as her mother told her on her deathbed to not worry about her passing, for she would come back to see her as a redbird. While Christians do not believe in reincarnation, I do believe God comforts those who mourn and that sending a redbird to the grieving person does not seem out of the realm of possibility. Interestingly enough, when her mother was in hospice, my friend told me a redbird was perched on the window sill through most of her mother's final hours. Since her mother's death, numerous redbirds have visited my friend, providing comfort.

Before Christmas, I told myself I must look up the meaning of the redbird. What does it symbolize for us Christians? I found the redbird, or red cardinal, specifically, has become a symbol of beauty and warmth of the holiday season. It is nature's reminder for us to focus on our faith. The cardinal's scarlet plumage represents the blood of Christ shed for the redemption of mankind. Isaiah 1:18 says, *Come now, let us settle the matter, says the LORD. Though your sins are like scarlet, they shall be as white as snow...*

Now I understand why it seemed God was tapping me on the shoulder before Christmas, saying, "Don't forget the redbird," as I bustled around shopping frantically. He told me, "Lisa, don't forget what this season is all about. It's also about my Son and your Savior, Jesus Christ, and the sacrifice He made for you." A good reminder. In fact, I might just go and unwrap one of those redbird ornaments and display it all year long.

Lisa Burkhardt Worley is a former national sports reporter and founder of Pearls of Promise Ministries. You can find her at *pearlsofpromiseministries.com.* Lisa is also the co-author of the award winning manuscript, *If I Only Had...Following God's Path to Your Security.*

Earl and Daddy

John Shackelford, Psy.D.

Many are the plans in a man's heart, but it is the Lord's purpose that prevails (Proverbs 19:21).

Thirteen year old Ginger left quickly at the end of our counseling session. An hour later I noticed her billfold between the cushions. The family lived out of town, and she would need her billfold. I was irritated at the inconvenience. Then I remembered her mother worked at the nursing home nearby. I could drop it off for her mom and be out in two minutes.

Buzzing through the double doors, I hurried down the hall toward the nursing station. As I glanced at patient names on the doors, one name caught my attention, Earl Flanary. My pace slowed. Earl Flanary. I stopped, as in some kind of memory trance. I pictured big Earl in farmer overalls. He was a childhood friend of my dad.

Memories of my dad and Earl flooded back. I recalled a day when I was nine years old and sat in church with Dad. The preacher asked everyone to come forward who wanted to know Jesus. I wanted to be "saved," but was afraid to walk the aisle. I quickly devised an alternate plan. My plan was to "be good enough" to go to heaven and avoid that intimidating walk with everyone looking.

Another day Dad and I did chores. He said going to heaven wasn't about being good. "My friend, Earl, is a really good man," he said. "He'd give you the shirt off his back. But he's not a Christian. He has no assurance of heaven."

I was sad and concerned for Earl. Next, I realized my "be good enough" plan wouldn't fly. So, I chose to walk that scary aisle with my sister. Nine years after that decisive day, Dad died of a heart attack.

Several years later I learned that Earl trusted Christ.

"Can I help you?" The aide's voice snapped me back to the present.

"Yes, I want to visit Earl Flanary," I heard myself say.

Entering the ninety-year-old's room, I touched his shoulder, "Earl, it's John Shackelford."

His eyes opened quickly and he flashed a warm smile of recognition. After asking how he was doing, we chatted about old times. As I prepared to go, an idea came to mind. After all, if you can't ask a personal favor of a man who loved your father, who can you ask?

"Earl," I said, and his gaze met mine, "Would you do me a favor?"

He looked puzzled so I went on, "Earl, when you get to heaven, would you say 'Hello' to my daddy?"

Earl said, "I will."

Leaving the nursing home that day, I smiled and realized that Ginger forgetting her billfold was no accident. It was God's clever way of leading me to Earl Flanary. Two weeks later, I heard that Earl had passed and felt confident he delivered my message.

I bet my daddy smiled too.

Dr. Shackelford practices psychology in Richardson and Glen Rose, Texas. His website is *ADHDTherapyDallasTBI.com*. He is a contributing author to *Christian Counseling Ethics*, co-authoring a chapter on "Abuse of Power." Areas of interest include ADHD diagnosis and integrating spiritual growth with psychotherapy.

My Pearl Necklace

Mary Jane Downs

After years of challenges, disappointments, and despair, I began to cry out to the Lord. I asked Him if I would ever get to the place where I could really witness for Him. I wondered about this because it seemed everything I did failed.

The Lord responded to my cry with the picture of a pearl necklace in my mind's eye and began to speak gently to my spirit.

"You are troubled by the circumstances you have gone through in your life. I have been with you through each and every one of them. And now I am working with you to help you see each of those lessons in a new way. I designed this spiritual pearl necklace especially for you. The pearls represent each situation you have experienced and overcome by My guidance and power. Just like the oyster suffers pain in growth, you have suffered pain in growth. The oyster covered his pain with something priceless. You have learned to cover your pain with something priceless as well—my glory and wisdom. Now I am lining up these experiences and putting a knot between each one so that you don't lose any of them. As you learn to wear this spiritual pearl necklace humbly, I will use you greatly."

Then I was lead to a verse in Matthew about the pearl of great price and the meaning became clear.

Again, the kingdom of heaven is like a merchant seeking fine pearls, and upon finding one pearl of great value, he went and sold all that he had and bought it (Matthew 13:45-46).

When we finally see Christ for who He is and realize His principles are true, then we will do whatever it takes to make sure they become a part of our life.

Having this spiritual necklace reminds me that all is not lost and God intends to use everything I go through for His glory. Even when I get off track, God makes the journey useful for me and for Him. Nothing is wasted and that brings me peace of mind.

How about your pearls that came at a great price? Will you allow God to line them up and show you off? God is so proud of you and your accomplishments for Him. You may feel at times that nothing ever goes right and that you have nothing to offer. Don't despair! God is still planning on using you as part of His witness in the future. Wait and see.

Mary Jane Downs is a writer and blogger from the foothills of Asheville, North Carolina. Her blog: *Joy in the Morning*, can be found at *maryjanewrites.com*.

Pearls of
Praise

The Ministry of Music

Marilyn Hurlbut

About midnight, Paul and Silas were praying and singing hymns to God, and the other prisoners were listening to them (Acts 16:25).

The place was Mozambique, Africa, and I lay on a bed wracked with fever and delirious. I didn't know how sick I was until later. I have no memory of ten days.

But my sister remembers. It was she who sat by my bedside, applying her early nurses' training and praying for my recovery. She told me that during this time she sang to me; in fact she sang through the entire Cokesbury Hymnal.

And then she said, "I was surprised at how many of the hymns you knew, because you would sing along with me." What a shock! I have no memory of doing this. And I'm a terrible singer. Apparently I sang while delirious or semi-conscious.

Now, in retrospect, I realize that all those hymns were somewhere deep down inside me: hymns of praise, thankfulness, and petition. And I'm grateful for the years of church attendance, the years of singing songs that became embedded in my memory, so that when words failed me, when consciousness fled, I could still sing, "Great is thy Faithfulness" from some unknown level.

Music ministers: music stays with us, deep within our souls.

Father, thank you for giving us so many different ways to praise you and communicate with you. Help us use these different means as we seek to walk with you on a 24/7 basis.

Dr. Marilyn Hurlbut is an adjunct professor and a former Manager of training and development at ARCO Oil and Gas Company.

Since I Met You

Caroline Gavin

I will sing of the Lord's great love forever (Psalm 89:1).

More lovely is the sound
Of the birds in song,
Since I met You,
Since to You I belong.

More blue is the sky,
More brilliant the sun,
Since I met You,
Since I found the One.

More green is the grass,
More fragrant the flower,
Since I met You,
Since I feel Your power.

More refreshing the rain,
More delightful the breeze,
Since I met You,
My heart ever You please.

More joyful the tree,
More glorious the hill,
Since I met You,
My longings You fill.

More exuberant the music
Of the splashing waterfall,
Since I met You,
My All in all.

More delightful each day,
More restful each night,
More lovely each moment,
More spectacular each sight.

More beautiful are all things,
Since I met You;
My Jesus, You beautify
All I say, think and do.

Your countenance radiant
Shines all 'round me;
Yea, the glory of Your face
Is in all I see.

The tenderness of Your touch
Ever do I feel,
Transcending my thought,
Yet ever true and real.

The music of Your voice
Resonates in all I hear,
Singing to my soul,
Ringing ever clear.

The captivating fragrance
Of You, the Sharon Rose,
I smell all around me
As my love ever grows.

Surely all things are lovely
Since You and I did meet;
Surely all things
You make divinely sweet.

So sing I shall of You,
And I offer You my life;
I proclaim Your praises
Through both joy and strife.

Your touch sweetens
Even seasons of pain;
Surely You bring Light
Even in the rain.

More lovely for You,
Beloved, I long to be;
I place all in Your hands,
Lord, take all of me.

Surrendered to You,
May I be fragrant as the flower,
As I yield all to You,
Embracing Your power.

For Your glory alone,
May I shine as the sun;
I live no longer for me,
But for You, Eternal One.

And since I met You I join
With the birds in song;
I sing of my Jesus,
To Whom I forever belong.

Caroline Gavin is a Christian life coach, speaker, author and host of Purposeful Pathway Radio. She is committed to helping others find their paths, live with purpose, and walk God's way. Refresh with her poetry at *PurposefulPathway.com* and in the forty-day poetic devotional book *Purposeful Pathway: Your Journey with Jesus.*

Through Jesus, therefore, let us continually offer to God a sacrifice of praise—the fruit of lips that openly profess his name.

— Hebrews 13:15

Out of the Box Praise

Angie McCoy

*A*s *the deer pants for streams of water, so my soul pants for you, my God* (Psalm 42:1).

I can remember scratching my head at Israel's belief that God—the Most High (Gen. 14:18)—dwelt in a temple, hidden away in the most holy of holies. What a silly thought: God, contained and restrained *in a box.*

You can guess where this is going, can't you?

Yes, I've put God in a box. More times than I care to admit. The size and shape of the box, remarkably, was the exact size and shape that I needed at the moment. I've put God in boxes marked "restorer" and boxes marked "teacher," boxes marked "comforter" and boxes marked "healer." Yes, over and over I reduced God to the size of my needs.

The truth is, we all do that. In fact, Scripture tells us that God *wants* to carry our burdens. *Do not be anxious about anything, but in every situation, by prayer and petition, with thanksgiving, present your requests to God* (Philippians 4:6).

Yet, because of our human condition, it's all too easy for us to view God solely through the narrow lens of our deficiencies and frailties. When we do that, it's like expecting nothing more from a sunrise than the absence of darkness. What are we missing?

Why don't we pursue God with our entire being, intent on trying to comprehend His might? Why, after we've been blessed by God to feel, to know, to experience a richer, deeper understanding of His character, do we inevitably allow our awe and praise of Him to dim?

Yes, we're invited to come before God with the desires of our hearts. And so we do, dropping to our knees with heads bowed and hands cupped in front of us, earnestly and expectantly awaiting only those things God can give us: comfort, peace, freedom from fear, wisdom, discernment, wholeness.

Today, though, come before God in praise. Approach Him not with a bowed head and clasped hands, but with your face turned upward and hands stretched outward in praise. Why? Because He is *the living and true God* (I Thess. 1:9) ... *God of all mankind* (Jer. 32:27) ... *creator of heaven and earth* (Gen. 14:19) ... *the Master in heaven* (Col 4:1) ... *the great King above all Gods* (Ps. 95:3) ... *the Mighty One* (Isa. 33:21) ... *I AM WHO I AM* (Ex 3:14).

Because He is God.

Angie McCoy is a freelance business writer serving clients in a variety of industries. Before creating her own business, she worked for large companies such as Kimberly-Clark, where she managed corporate communications, oversaw executive communications, and created and wrote online newsletters.

See the Son

Lori Wildenberg

"They just got a new house." "Her husband surprised her with a trip for their anniversary." "She just found out she's pregnant."

Don't get me wrong. I'm not a bitter person. I'm sincerely happy for people when good things come their way. But when times in my life are more of a struggle than a blessing I wonder, "When is it my turn?"

That thought has the potential to morph into self-focused pity—the feeling of not being able to get out of bed or not wanting to open the blinds to let in the sun.

But...God has shown me how to open my blind eyes and let in the Son.

Praise.

Praise God when you don't feel like it. In the book, *The Hiding Place,* Corrie Ten Boom talks about being a prisoner during World War II. Corrie's sister, Betsy, tells her to be thankful in all circumstances. Sarcastically, Corrie says she's going to thank God for the fleas. As it turns out, the insects had a purpose. Corrie and her sister were able to hold a Bible study in the German prison camp because the pests prevented the guards from entering the barracks.

I have found my flea-filled, heartbreaking situation may not change but when my focus is readjusted my thought process is transformed.

I can do this with God's help...but it isn't easy.

When the enemy gets God's people to only see themselves in comparison to others, their joy is stolen.

Enough of that! Are you with me? Grab it back! Praise God for who He is. Thank Him for what He has done. Choose to see the many blessings in front of you and respond with a grateful heart. Life is full of unexpected challenges and blessings. During those times that are consumed with disappointment, first honestly cry out and then start praising God.

Praise is the best offensive weapon against despair .

Do not be anxious about anything, but in every situation, by prayer and petition, with thanksgiving, present your requests to God. And the peace of God, which transcends all understanding, will guard your hearts and your minds in Christ Jesus (Philippians 4:6-7).

How have you dealt with life's disappointments? How have those disappointments affected your relationships with the Lord?

Lori Wildenberg is co-founder of 1 Corinthians 13 Parenting and parenting co-columnist for *Marriage Magazine*. Lori is co-author of *EMPOWERED PARENTS: Putting Faith First* and a contributor to many other books. Visit *loriwildenberg.com* or *1Corinthians13Parenting.com* for more information.

In Need of a Savior

Catherine Weiskopf

Growing up as a good girl, obedience ruled my life. I was afraid to whisper in class or be late for school. Even at home I wore the label of a "good girl." My sister demanded more and yelled louder, while I ate spaghetti that was rotten without complaining, never stayed out too late, never cussed, and only once raised my voice at my mother.

But being a "good girl" carries with it all sorts of problems. It is tempting for us who go around with halos on to not see our sin clearly. The more I saw myself as good, the less I needed a savior.

Fortunately, the more I studied the Bible and got to know God and His holiness, the more I saw the truth about myself. As Jesus said, *"You have heard that it was said to the people long ago, 'You shall not murder, and anyone who murders will be subject to judgment.' But I tell you that anyone who is angry with a brother or sister will be subject to judgment"* (Matthew 5:21-22).

Some people need a savior for their outsides first. They need Jesus to help them clean up the messes they have made. Their sin regurgitates over so many people that no pretense is plausible. Others of us look very calm and together on the outside. (I personally suffered from anxiety problems for years and no one except my husband knew because my facial expression never changed even in the middle of a severe anxiety attack.) But I still need a savior for the inside.

I need a savior to clean out the garbage inside.

I need a savior to keep me at peace.

I need a savior to atone for my inside sins that only Jesus knows about.

I need a savior to set me free, step by step, from every thought that holds me captive.

As it says in Romans 3:23: *for all have sinned and fall short of the glory of God.* How wonderful it is that Jesus is our personal Savior: a Savior who died for both outside and inside sinners.

Then He turned toward the woman and said to Simon, Do you see this woman? I came into your house. You did not give me any water for my feet, but she wet my feet with her tears and wiped them with her hair. You did not give me a kiss, but this woman, from the time I entered, has not stopped kissing my feet. You did not put oil on my head, but she has poured perfume on my feet. Therefore, I tell you, her many sins have been forgiven—as her great love has shown. But whoever has been forgiven little loves little (Luke 7:44-47).

Catherine Weiskopf is the creative director of POP Ministries. She is a Christian and educational writer dedicated to helping others tell their stories. She is the co-author of the award winning manuscript, *If I Only Had... Following God's Path to Your Security,* and is currently co-authoring two Bible studies. Contact her at *cweiskopf@pearlsofpromiseministries.com.*

Where Can You Find God?

Lisa Burkhardt Worley

I have always realized the importance of praising God, but I will confess I am a closet "praiser." I am not one to raise my hands in church toward the heavens nor am I one to vocally shout "Praise God!" when there is an answered prayer. However, I do praise God at home on bended knee every day and I love to listen to Christian contemporary music inside my home while I'm cleaning the house.

What I realized is that I did not see the bigger picture concerning praise. When we praise God, we draw Him nearer to us. Psalm 22:3 in the King James Version states, *But thou art holy, O thou that inhabitest the praises of Israel.* God lives in our praises! Praising the Lord is a cure for spiritual dryness. When David was fleeing from King Saul, he was fearful for his life, hiding out in caves, hungry and thirsty, but in Psalm 63:1-4 he praises God despite his circumstances:

O God, you are my God, earnestly I seek you; my soul thirsts for you, my body longs for you, in a dry and weary land where there is no water. I have seen you in the sanctuary and beheld your power and your glory. Because your love is better than life, my lips will glorify you. I will praise you as long as I live....

As I read this, I realized that if God seems distant at any time, I can find Him by praising Him! When we bless the Lord through our words, raise our hands in praise to the Lord or sing to the Lord, it's an invitation to God to fill us and inhabit our praises.

This concept reminded me of an experience 16 years ago. I was driving in my car from Stratford, Connecticut, to Boston, Massachusetts, when I popped in a tape with the song, "Have I Told You Lately" on it. As I listened to the words, I thought, "Wow, that is a very spiritual song!" I began to sing it at the top of my lungs over and over to God.

What happened after that day was amazing! Almost everywhere I went, the song "Have I Told You Lately" played. It played when I was at the grocery store. It played when I was at the drug store. It played at the restaurants I went to. My praises had brought God very near, so close that I could almost touch Him. For me, the message is, I need to get back to the business of praising God. I had become lax in it and because of that, I had become spiritually dry at times. Remember the words of Psalm 43:5: *Why, my soul, are you downcast? Why so disturbed within me? Put your hope in God, for I will yet praise Him, my Savior and my God.*

Praise God! He is worthy to be praised!

Lisa Burkhardt Worley is a Christian motivational speaker and writer and is the founder of Pearls of Promise Ministries, *pearlsofpromiseministries.com*. She is the co-author of the award winning manuscript, *If I Only Had...Following God's Path to Your Security*, and is an editor for the *Pearls of Promise* devotional. Follow her on Twitter *@pearlsofpromise* or visit the POP Facebook page at */pearlsofpromiseministries*.

Protection

Trisha McWilliams

*B*ecause he loves me, says the Lord, I will rescue him;
I will protect him, for he acknowledges my name....
(Psalm 91:14).

In November 2004, my children and I were on the way to buy a new shirt for my oldest son Dalton's upcoming kindergarten school pictures. On the way, we stopped at a video store to rent a movie. We pulled into a front row parking space and Dalton got out of the truck and went to wait for me at the front door. I went to the passenger side to lift my younger son, Davin, 15 months old, out of his car seat.

Suddenly, a car sped up quickly, jumped the median, and headed straight for Blockbuster's front door. I froze as thoughts raced through my mind:

"Did we have time to move?"

"Or should we stay still?"

"Where was Dalton?"

"If it hits we will be killed."

Before I could finish these thoughts, the vehicle came whizzing by us and hit the storefront at a high speed. It missed our vehicle by about three feet.

Then reality hit. A vehicle had just crashed into this store, glass was shattered and scattered everywhere. Davin was still buckled in his car seat. I knew he was safe because he was right with me. Where was Dalton? Panic rushed through my body. All I could see was broken glass everywhere.

"Dalton," I screamed.

My eyes rested upon him safe and sound still standing in front of the store. The glass that shattered surrounded him.

"Mom, I saw glass fly by my head," he told me still dazed by the accident.

I knew emergency crews would be arriving soon so I moved the truck into another space on the side of the store. As we got in the truck, the Lord's presence was thick and heavy as He spoke to me. He said, "Look at how I protect you."

You see, I had been reverently praying for His protection over each one of us, especially my children. I had been praying for Him to protect each of us from harm, sickness, and injury. The reality of what could have happened set in. My whole body shook as I sobbed with thankfulness. There was no other explanation as to why we were completely unharmed other than God's protection.

I felt there were 1,000 angels surrounding my truck during the accident and I felt a closeness to my Lord I had not experienced in a long time. God proved to me that day how big and powerful He was and that He does answer prayers!

Trisha McWilliams is the assistant director of an early learning center in Flower Mound, Texas, and is the co-leader of a ministry at her church that reaches young moms called "The MOBB" (Mothers of Babies and Big Kids).

Close Call

Tom Blubaugh

My eyes flew open as I looked at the clock! I was going to be late to class! Hurrying into the bathroom, I ran my hand over my face. *Prickly.* After quickly shaving and a fast shower, I headed out the door with my briefcase in one hand and toast in the other. It was a dreary fall morning in Kansas City. I climbed into the car and was glad to hear the motor turn over at first try. I backed out of the driveway and headed for I-435.

I was married with two sons ages six and three at the time. I worked full-time as an insurance agent, was active in my church, and took twelve hours of Bible courses. I knew the boys would be in bed by the time I got home.

By the time I reached the I-435 on-ramp, fog surrounded me. I could only see taillights. I turned on the radio and clutched the steering wheel. Christian music calmed my nerves.

The fog had gotten thicker by the time I reached the Missouri River. No taillights appeared in front of me so I glanced down at the speedometer: *50 mph.* "Maybe a little too fast for the conditions," I thought so I took my foot off the gas.

When I looked up, there was a clear patch in front of me, and then the red taillight of a car too close!!!

No time for brakes!

I clenched the steering wheel, gritted my teeth, closed my eyes and waited for the impact!

Nothing! No crash! No sound of metal on metal!

I opened my eyes and stared out at the fog,

"What just happened?" I was shaking. "Thank you, Lord! What happened to that car? It didn't have time to change lanes! Did I go through it? Over it? Were there angels? Wow!"

That incident took place thirty-eight years ago and I still don't have an explanation of what happened that day. I've praised and thanked God numerous times for sparing me and whoever was in the other car. I hope the Lord will show me what occurred that morning someday when I get to heaven.

Have mercy on me, my God, have mercy on me, for in you I take refuge, I will take refuge in the shadow of your wings until the disaster has passed (Psalm 57:1).

Tom Blubaugh is the author of *Night of the Cossack* and co-wrote *The Great Adventure*. Tom has been a public speaker for 40 years. You can find him at *tomblubaugh.net*.

God Will Make a Way

Caroline Gavin

See, I am doing a new thing! Now it springs up; do you not perceive it? I am making a way in the wilderness and streams in the wasteland (Isaiah 43:19).

When the path is foggy,
When my way is unclear,
When the storms begin to rage,
When the darkness is near—

Surely it seems
That I will not make it through;
Surely it seems hope is gone—
Yet then I see You.

You will make a way, Lord,
When there is no way at all;
You will make a way, Lord,
And lift me when I fall.

When trials overwhelm me,
When I am too weary to move,
You will make a way, Lord,
Your mercy You will prove.

You lift me in Your arms,
You carry me when I am weak;
You shine light upon my path,
You give the words to speak.

Tenderly You wipe
Streaming tears from my eyes;
Gently You lift my head,
You point upward to the skies.

You remind me that the sun
Shines even when clouds do loom;
You remind me that You arose,
You left behind an empty tomb.

What have I to worry then
When You, my Lord, are near?
What have I to worry?
Whom have I to fear?

For my Jesus is with me,
My God will make a way;
The night He will turn to light
Shining as the bright of day.

Yea, God will make a way
When there is no way at all;
God will make a way
And lift me when I fall.

I know surely in the storm
I will make it through;
For You are here with me—
And all I need is You.

You light my path,
You make my way clear;
So I rejoice even in the storms,
For my sweet Jesus is here.

Caroline Gavin is a Christian life coach, speaker, author and host of Purposeful Pathway Radio. She is committed to helping others find their paths, live with purpose, and walk God's way. Refresh with her poetry at *PurposefulPathway.com* and in the forty-day poetic devotional book *Purposeful Pathway: Your Journey with Jesus.*

The Exercise Bike

Lisa Burkhardt Worley

Can I tell you a secret? My husband was given an exercise bike for his birthday. He thinks it's his bike, for his enjoyment or torture, depending on how you look at it. However, I'm benefitting from his gift in an amazing way! Shhh....don't tell him his present is for me as well.

This past week, I hauled my praise music upstairs, opened up the blinds so I could see God's beautiful creation and began to sing and praise God for thirty minutes on the bike's "fat burner" setting. It was a special time alone with God, letting Him know how much I loved Him and how I appreciated His direction in my life. Before I knew it, I had run the course on the stationary bike and already looked forward to the next block of time.

We don't have to earmark church for our praise and worship of the Lord. We can praise Him while exercising, we can praise Him while driving, and we can worship Him while doing mundane tasks at home. When I need to clean house, I crank up the praise music to make the process more enjoyable!

Psalm 100:4 encourages us to: *Enter His gates with thanksgiving and His courts with praise; give thanks to Him and praise His name.* Before we ever seek God out with our prayer concerns, we need to praise Him first. Plug praise into your GPS and it'll navigate you right to God!

The creator of the universe deserves our praise. Will you take the time today to tell Him how great and magnificent He is?

Lisa Burkhardt Worley is a Christian motivational speaker and writer and is the founder of Pearls of Promise Ministries, *pearlsofpromiseministries.com*. She is the co-author of *If I Only Had...Following God's Path to Your Security*, and is an editor for the *Pearls of Promise* devotional. Follow her on Twitter *@pearlsofpromise*.

. . . .
. . . .
. . . .

Pearls of Prayer

Restored In God's Presence

Kathy R. Green

On my morning walks I always enjoy passing by the beautiful pond in my neighborhood. The reflection of the sun settling on the still waters as the ducks rest on the lush green grass reminds me of the Psalm of David—*He makes me to lie down in green pastures; He leads me beside still waters. He restores my soul...*(Psalm 23:2-3a, ESV). As I pause to reflect on the beauty of God's creation, peace and tranquility flood my heart and the cares of the world seem to disappear, until the activities of the day beckon me to move on.

The world is moving faster than ever before, and we can easily become overwhelmed by the pressures of life as we strive to meet all the demands that are placed on our time. And besides our normal day-to-day activities, there are times when we find ourselves in a place of turmoil due to a bad report from the doctor, or the loss of someone dear, or a perpetual problem in our marriage and family that continues to weigh us down. So what do we do when life has robbed us of our peace and joy? How do we cope and keep ourselves from losing it altogether?

When God allows us to face difficult situations, it's only to teach us how to trust Him. While these seasons of heartache, disappointment, and frustration are designed by Satan to defeat us and cause us to lose hope, God uses them for His greater glory. When life presses hard against us, the Word tells us to simply be still and know that He is God. If we yield to the gentle leading of the Holy Spirit as He draws us to the place of prayer, we will find rest and restoration for our weary soul.

For thus says the Lord God: *In returning and rest you shall be saved; in quietness and confidence shall be your strength* (Isaiah 30:15 ESV). God has provided us a safe and quiet place called the secret place, where we can fellowship with Him, and learn to rest in His ability to care for us. Only when we settle ourselves and cease from our worries and frustrations are we restored by God's presence. As we fellowship with God day by day He brings us back to a state of peace and soundness of mind, and He gives us strength to carry on.

David, the young shepherd boy, understood the role of the shepherd as well as He understood sheep, which is so beautifully displayed in the 23rd Psalm. Just as He watched over the sheep and protected them from the lion and bear that threatened to destroy them, he knew God would watch over him and protect him in times of trouble. David declared the Lord to be his shepherd. When we find ourselves frustrated, confused, and overcome by the pressures of life, we must be still and rest in God, where we will find safety from the storm, peace, and restoration for our soul.

Kathy R. Green is the author of two books, *Pray-ers Bear Fruit* and *Come*. You can find her at *KathyRGreen.com*.

Guiding Lights

Jennifer Mersberger

I have a strong dislike of driving in the rain. That dislike is only surpassed by driving in the rain in the dark. So you can imagine my excitement when the sky opened up and began to pour as I dropped my daughter off at school at 5:00 on a Saturday morning for a volleyball tournament.

Prayers for safety began flowing out of me like water. I could barely see a thing and was continuously blinded by the oncoming traffic. *Please God, be my eyes. Please take me safely home.* My hands clenched the steering wheel as I rigidly focused on the unlit road ahead of me. A large semi-truck sped past, pulled into my lane and cruised along a few car lengths ahead. The lights on the back of that semi were all I could see and they guided me through the steady rain. When I saw the lights swerve, I knew I would need to swerve with the road too. When his brake lights lit up, I slowed my car down with him. For several miles I mimicked the driver's actions. Soon I was at my exit and we parted ways.

I merged into the traffic on the frontage road. Traffic consisted of one car. I once again followed the taillights as we traveled the dark roads together. When the car reached its destination and turned off the road, the rain stopped. God had led me through the storm.

What storms are you in the midst of right now? God's word promises that He is there with you. He will not leave you! Pray that you will see a glimpse of Him in the midst of your storm and then trust His plan for you. Our God is mighty and can conquer your storm! Until He does, allow Him to guide you home.

The Lord Himself goes before you and will be with you; He will never leave you nor forsake you. Do not be afraid; do not be discouraged (Deuteronomy 31:8).

Jennifer Mersberger is an Amazon Top 15 Christian author, public speaker, and founder of Lamplight Ministry. Through her Bible studies and weekly blog, Jennifer uses her unique perspective and fun sense of humor to help you see God in your everyday. Get to know her at *lamplightministry.com* and *Facebook.com/JenniferMersberger*.

God's Faithful Answer to Prayer

Kaye Sandridge

My husband and I agreed before having children, we would raise them with a knowledge and faith in God. Raising my young children to trust in God was challenging as I was equally young in my faith walk, but as I stumbled forward, I was encouraged by a Bible study leader to give God opportunities to show His faithfulness to our family.

At the end of our vacation, my opportunity came. My four-year-old daughter had the unexpected joy of making a friend during our week long stay. The two had spent hours playing in the pool and at the park. On the afternoon of our departure she said, "Mom, I never got to say good-bye to my friend." A sad feeling came over me as I recalled hearing they were supposed to leave earlier in the day. I had been too busy to think my daughter would want to express her appreciation to the one who brought her hours of enjoyment. As we drove to the condo office to turn in our keys, I asked my daughter to say a prayer with me that their plans changed so she could see her friend again. While we prayed for that moment to happen, I said my own silent prayer for God to show is faithfulness to her by answering her prayer. I wish I could tell you my faith was deep enough to know all would work out, but it wasn't.

As we pulled into the office parking lot, we experienced great joy when we saw my daughter's friend and her family just checking out! My daughter got to say her sweet good-bye and to my delight, we then got to thank our Father for answering both our prayers. It was a beautiful display of God's love to us!

Mark 11:24: *Therefore I tell you, whatever you ask for in prayer, believe that you have received it, and it will be yours.*

Kaye Sandridge is a ministry leader at her church, Trietsch Memorial United Methodist Church, Flower Mound, Texas.

His Eye Is on the Sparrow

Marilyn Hurlbut

For I am convinced that neither death nor life ... will be able to separate us from the love of God that is in Christ Jesus our Lord (Romans 8:38-39).

These days, my sister-in-law's name is a permanent fixture on my prayer list. She's showing signs of Alzheimer's disease, and all of us feel sad. Since she was diagnosed six months ago, I've thought often of Alzheimer's and cringed when I, myself, showed any of the symptoms. Getting lost while driving, for example, which I've done all my life, is now accompanied by a twinge of panic and the inner thought, "Uh, oh; is this the beginning? Will I too end up with Alzheimer's?"

But recently, as I've prayed for my sister-in-law, it's dawned on me that Alzheimer's, hers or possibly mine in the future, doesn't matter all that much, because God's love is still there. "I am convinced," said the apostle Paul, "Nothing can separate us from the love of God which is in Christ Jesus our Lord." That means Alzheimer's, cancer, dementia, stroke, heart disease—all things we fear as we grow older—none of these will diminish God's great love for us. We think these diseases are tragic, but God may have another perspective.

God loves at the soul level which transcends the physical in ways we don't yet understand. So whatever happens to our bodies—and even to our minds—we will still be loved. We will still be able to worship Him in spirit and in truth— the truth we will eventually understand.

We are loved by the One whose eye is on the sparrow. My sister-in-law is in good hands. And we are too. No matter what.

Dr. Marilyn Hurlbut is an adjunct professor and a former manager of training and development at ARCO Oil and Gas Company.

God Provides the Answers

Kris Benson

Pray and Listen! I live by these two actions. As a principal of a large elementary school I am constantly put in situations where people look to me for answers and guidance. I learned, while being a counselor, that I did not have the answers so I'd better pray. Before I walk into a tough meeting I learned to pray, "Lord, give me the words they need to hear, not what I want to say!" I pray this prayer and then calm myself and listen to God. I can't tell you how many times God has been the hero in my office!

Last week, I met with a family where the parents were divorced. The ex-wife, ex-husband, and step-mom all knew each other because they used to be in the same Sunday School class at church. The tension was high to say the least! I prayed my prayer and sure enough, God gave me the words they all needed to hear to help their children.

This week I had a third grade boy end up in my office because he hit a girl and bit another. I was frustrated because he has ended up in my office five times over the last two weeks. I wanted to "dish out a consequence equal to the crime." I prayed and asked God to give me the words he needed to hear, not what I wanted to say. God dissolved my anger and gave me words. Within twenty minutes he had shared with me all that was happening in his life, which was HUGE, and I quickly discovered what was behind his anger.

The family is now in counseling and they are receiving the help they need.

I have yet to find a situation where this prayer hasn't worked. God knows the answers and He wants to use us to help the situation. Pray, listen and then give God the credit.

For the Holy Spirit will teach you at that time what you should say (Luke 12:12).

Kris Benson has been an educator for over twenty years.

Power in Prayer

Caroline Gavin

Pray without ceasing (1 Thessalonians 5:17, KJV).

On my knees before You
I approach You in prayer,
I sense Your presence, Lord,
I know You are near.

Your radiant face
Shines in my mind's eye;
You are the Source of life,
For me You chose to die.

All my trials, my Jesus,
I release unto You,
So too all my victories
I place on the altar too.

Everything is Yours,
As my life You bought;
When You shed Your blood,
It was me You sought.

How can I not then follow
When I hear You call?
All I must release
To You, my All in all.

Everything You give me,
I then give You everything;
Enthroned in my heart,
Forever You are my King.

The power of Your Cross
Bridges Your heart and mine;
Your blood washes my sin,
'Tis the fount of life divine.

Before You now I kneel,
I humbly bow my head;
Thank You, precious Savior,
That for my life You bled.

To the foot of Your Cross
I travel in my mind;
No stronger, sweeter love
Ever will I find.

Calvary is on my heart
When I am on bended knee;
I see my sweet Jesus
Bleeding on the tree.

Come here often, Lord,
Yea, I vow to do;
Kneeling here in prayer
I am all the closer to You.

Radiant is Your face,
Sparkling with love Your eye;
How I love You, Jesus,
For me You chose to die.

Your presence, Lord, I feel,
I know You are near;
On my knees before You
I feel Your power in prayer.

Caroline Gavin is a Christian life coach, speaker, author and host of Purposeful Pathway Radio. She is committed to helping others find their paths, live with purpose, and walk God's way. Refresh with her poetry at *PurposefulPathway.com* and in the forty-day poetic devotional book, *Purposeful Pathway: Your Journey with Jesus.*

Being Honest With God

Marilyn Hurlbut

*H*ow long must I wrestle with my thoughts and every day have sorrow in my heart? (Psalm 13:2)

The words poured out of me onto the pages of my prayer journal, "Dear Lord, I come to you this morning with furrowed brow and heavy heart. I'm having difficulty remembering lightness, happiness, contentment. But no trouble at all reliving hurt, anger, depression."

"I'm playacting everywhere—with you above all—trying to act devout, following routines of prayer and Scripture reading, but feeling so much doubt and emptiness."

"I'm glad for the habit of starting each day with you. I miss this hour with you when I don't honor the habit. But I'm NOT glad when I cannot sense your presence, when even spiritual disciplines seem meaningless and rote and I am still full of myself and my own ego. Give me back a sense of you. As with Gideon of old, I throw out a sponge and wait for a sign. Are you really there? Are you real?"

Then Hebrews 11 floats in from somewhere. *Faith is being sure of what we hope for, certain of what we cannot see.* I know this verse. But right now I know it only in my head and not in my heart. And even this verse is not especially comforting. It will be tomorrow maybe. But not today. So at this moment, Lord, the best I can do is thank you for tomorrow, for the change I know will come at some future time.

Dr. Marilyn Hurlbut is an adjunct professor and a former manager of training and development at ARCO Oil and Gas Company.

Prayer Envy

Anne Marie Davis

Prayer envy. I had it bad. I remember years ago walking away from a Bible study feeling irritable and a little angry. Someone had requested prayer for something frivolous for her house. It wasn't a necessity, and she put a dollar amount to it—one that I found astronomical. I silently fumed over that prayer request because due to overwhelming medical bills at the time, I was just hoping we'd find the money to pay for new tires for my car.

Two weeks later, this woman reported back that God answered her prayer. It was creatively answered, too. In retrospect, it was an amazing story, but at the time, I was annoyed. Why was God answering her prayer for something she didn't even need when so many people had desperate pleas for necessities that were seemingly unanswered?

Years later, when I had better perspective and a bit more maturity, I saw things very differently. This woman had a very big prayer need, a different one from what she'd asked for that day. Someone's eternity at stake. Years later, it was still unanswered. What do we do in those situations? Jesus tells us in Luke 11 to be like the person who persistently asks his friend for bread for his guests until the friend *finally* opens the door and gives it to him. Our prayers are to be like that. But it can feel like being left in the desert alone if God doesn't answer our prayers in a timely (from our perspective) manner. We're impatient, and impatience can lead to a paucity of faith.

I can't know for sure why God chose to answer what

I saw as a frivolous prayer request. But I suspect it had to do with helping her keep her faith. Her main prayer need was real and serious, and to this day, it remains unanswered. But perhaps by giving her that thing she wanted for her home, the Lord was telling her, "I hear you." He knows our needs, He loves us, He hears us, and He blesses us. How He does this is unique to each person and situation, and being envious is a fruitless endeavor that can lead to bitterness. I should have rejoiced that my friend's prayer was answered, regardless of how I viewed the request.

Those tires I needed back then? We found the money. The Lord took care of us, too. I'd love to say that I rejoiced and thanked God profusely, but I genuinely can't remember if I did. Obviously, the Lord had a lot of work to do on my heart at that time. Thankfully, He is patient with me, even though I'm often not patient with Him. He gives to each of us according to our need, and that is cause for joy. *Humble yourselves, therefore, under God's mighty hand, that He may lift you up in due time. Cast all your anxiety on Him because He cares for you* (1 Peter 5:6-7).

Anne Marie Davis is a displaced Texan now living in Bartlesville, OK, with her husband, son, and two spoiled cats.

The Encounter

Sally Metzger

I flew out of bed at the sound of Brian's chilling screams. My five-year-old had his share of bad dreams, but this was different. The air in his room seemed charged with fear.

"It's okay, honey." I sat on Brian's bed and gently patted his hands. "It's just a nightmare. Mommy is right here."

Brian's body remained stiff with terror. I turned on the light. I kissed his cheek and carried him to the rocker. Brian was inconsolable.

It occurred to me that I should pray; in fact, I should pray aloud. In the same moment I had the opposite inclination. What if I prayed and God did nothing? After all, Brian was just learning about God. I needed to protect his young faith against the slings and arrows of outrageous life. Sometimes God's "mysterious ways" made me doubt his providence altogether.

"It's okay, honey. Really." I sighed and hushed in motherly tones: "Shhhhhh, it's okay, baby."

Still Brian's fear remained.

"Sweetheart, let's talk to God about this," I said feebly. "Dear God," I began.

Between the "Dear" and the "God" of my salutation, Brian's little body went limp with peace. My prayer wasn't powerful, memorable, or well-spoken—a lackluster string of words—but it didn't matter. The moment, the meeting, belonged to my son and God. My prayer trailed off with a final "Amen."

As I rocked my peaceful child, I realized I'd had a wakeup call. Not Brian's terrified screams in the middle of the night, but a wakeup call concerning my own lack of faith. I had, after all, been afraid to pray out loud with my son. I'd had so little trust that God would come through for us. In addition, it seemed I was interpreting the struggles in my life as some sign of abandonment. When God's answers weren't what I'd hoped for, I felt He hadn't answered at all.

Brian stretched, repositioned himself in my arms, and laid his head back on my shoulder. I let the warmth of his body comfort me. I had so much to learn, so much growing to do. I silently prayed as the father in Mark 9:24: *Lord, I believe; help my unbelief* (ESV). For good measure, I added, "and Lord, help it be sooner rather than later, so that I can support this little one in his faith walk."

How amazing, I thought, that God had responded so quickly to my plea for help. It gave me chills, despite the warm little body snuggled up to me.

Brian interrupted my musings as he sat upright in my lap. His eyes wide with wonder, his little voice solemn with awe, Brian whispered, "Mommy, how did He get here so quick?"

Sally Metzger, M.T.S. is a Dallas speaker and spiritual director who seeks to help others deepen intimacy with God. Sally taught theology at Jesuit College Preparatory School of Dallas for 21 years and is currently writing a book on Ignatian Spirituality. Visit *sallymetzgerauthor.com.*

She Prayed for Me

Lisa Burkhardt Worley

I recently returned from the annual college women's retreat I co-lead with a former classmate. Spiritual in nature, our theme was "Connecting the Dots in Relationships." Our goal was not only to reconnect with the women we went to college with but to also reconnect with God. One of the women attending the retreat for the first time was my big sister in the sorority I pledged. Her memories of me in college probably weren't all that positive. I was a loud, energetic athlete who didn't miss any parties and admittedly had my priorities upside down. As I recall, there was a reason to drink almost every night, and my studies, and probably my sports endeavors, suffered the first couple of years of college.

I spent some time chatting with my sorority sister and told her I had a turning point in my life that set me on a different path, leading to Christ. I began to tell her about my transformation story that happened in my early thirties. After I shared, she told me that in college she had become disappointed with all the partying going on at school so she pulled back from the crowd and began to pray for people. She said that I was one of the ones she prayed for in college and continued to pray for throughout the years. I was dumbfounded! Someone was praying for me over the years? It brought tears to my eyes as I have to believe my friend's prayers most likely contributed to the reason my life made a U-turn into the right direction.

I began to realize that it took about 15 years before the prayers for me were answered, and many more years before my friend saw the fruit of her prayers in action at our annual retreat! A lesson for all of us is to be persistent in prayer, even if we don't see results right away. Mark 21:22 says, *If you believe, you will receive whatever you ask for in prayer.* My friend believed only God could turn my life around and the lives of the others she prayed for. God blessed her for her diligence that took root in her as a young woman in college.

How about you? Are you interceding for those in your life who have gone astray? Prayer is one of the most powerful ways to bring them back.

Lisa Burkhardt Worley is a former national television sports reporter, now Christian motivational speaker and founder of Pearls of Promise Ministries. She is the co-author of the award winning manuscript, *If I Only Had...Following God's Path to Your Security and* is a co-editor of the *Pearls of Promise* devotional. Follow her on Twitter *@pearlsofpromise.*

Pearls of Love

I Love You So Much!

Rebecca Carrell

CRASH! BANG! "Mommmmmmmyyy!"

As a mother of a five and six year old, the preceding scenario is a familiar one. It seems as though at least once a day, one of my children is falling off a couch, a bike, or a scooter, which cause both a fright and an attention-demanding boo-boo.

How I love this stage. The stage where only a mommy's kiss can fix it.

The trauma is not always physical. Yesterday it was my son who came racing toward me, sobbing uncontrollably, tears streaming down his face. My daughter and our neighbor's two children didn't want to play the game that Nick did, and the play-date quickly unraveled.

I scooped my son up in my arms and held him close. "Oh honey, I love you so much. Mommy loves you so much. Shhhh." After a few minutes, my son calmed down enough to talk about it, and we found a solution.

Later in the day my daughter and I were on a bike ride when a sharp turn and a pile of sand got the best of her and down she went. I raced over to her, gathered her in my arms, and calmed her down the same way: "I know, honey. I know. Come here. Mommy loves you so much." Moments later, we were on our way.

Later on, I sat pondering the day's events. How interesting that, no matter the occasion for tears, my immediate response is always the same. I gather them into my arms. I hold them as tight as I can, and I remind them over and over of my love for them. And the strangest thing about that is this: no matter the occasion for tears, *it is my love for them* that seems to comfort them the most.

John 15:9: *As the Father has loved me, so have I loved you. Now remain in my love.*

The night before He went to the cross, Jesus spent His remaining time illustrating His love for His disciples. His predominant concern seemed to be for their peace of mind. He warned them of trials and difficulties. He warned them of coming persecutions. And His solution was always the same: *Remain in my love.*

I will never be able to fix even a fourth of the problems my children will face. I have no intention of pretending that I can. If I could, I probably wouldn't. They need to learn how to resolve conflict in a mature and respectful manner. They must go through adversity to gain moral character. They must experience pain to gain compassion and empathy. They'll learn patience through persevering, and endurance through suffering.

I love them too much to rob them of that. But my promise to them, even at the tender ages of five and six, is that I will love them through *everything*. Their mistakes will never outweigh my love.

Sweet friend, how much more then, does the Father love you?

Rebecca Ashbrook Carrell has been a radio personality in the Dallas Ft. Worth area since 1998. She left full-time radio to found LSS Ministries but can still be heard on a part-time basis at Christian talk station 90.9 KCBI. Rebecca writes and teaches Bible studies and authors a devotional on her website, *LoveServeShine.com*.

The Greatest Commandment

Lisa Burkhardt Worley

About nine years ago, I was studying Deuteronomy in my Old Testament seminary class where we came across these famous biblical words known as the "Shema" in the Jewish culture. For the Jews, the words are an affirmation of Judaism and a declaration of faith in God:

Hear, O Israel: The LORD our God, the LORD is one. Love the LORD your God with all your heart and with all your soul and with all your strength. These commandments that I give you today are to be on your hearts. Impress them on your children. Talk about them when you sit at home and when you walk along the road, when you lie down and when you get up. Tie them as symbols on your hands and bind them on your foreheads. Write them on the doorframes of your houses and on your gates.

My professor noted some of these words are also in the New Testament. In Matthew, when Jesus is asked by an expert in the law to name the greatest commandment, He replies, *Love the Lord your God with all your heart and with all your soul and with all your mind.* If God thought these words were important enough to write on the doorframes and if Jesus thought it was the greatest commandment, then I needed to find a plaque with these words to post in my home. It would remind me daily of how I am to love God.

For two years I searched for this specific plaque. I looked at every Christian book store I came across and even checked for it online, but came up empty-handed. I asked a local Christian gift shop owner to see if she could find anything like this and she came back saying, "It simply doesn't exist." However, she had a thought. One of her vendors in Louisiana made custom plaques and was looking for something new, so she passed this option by the vendor. They loved the idea and created a beautiful plaque with the Shema on it. The first one ever produced is sitting above my door.

What does it mean to "Love the Lord your God with all your heart, soul and strength?" I believe you can compare it to the time you fell in love with your spouse. You wanted to spend all your time with them. Your thoughts were focused on them. You could not wait to see them. You wanted to learn everything about them so you studied them!

God wants us to feel the same way about Him. He wants our hearts to belong to Him. He wants us to spend time with Him every day in Bible study and in prayer. He desires our thoughts to be centered on Him.

Do you love the Lord your God with all your heart, soul and strength?

Lisa Burkhardt Worley is a former national television sports reporter, now Christian motivational speaker and writer and is the founder of Pearls of Promise Ministries, *pearlsofpromiseministries.com*. She is the co-author of the award winning manuscript, *If I Only Had…Following God's Path to Your Security* and is an editor for the *Pearls of Promise* devotional. Follow Lisa on Twitter *@pearlsofpromise*.

God Is Love

Lynn Macmillan

*D*o not fear, for I have redeemed you; I have sum-moned you by name, you are mine (Isaiah 43:1).

What is LOVE? I struggle with the concept.

God is LOVE! I struggle with that concept too.

It appears that LOVE is a constant thought about and concern for another.

If that is so, do I LOVE God?

Do I really think about anyone daily? I seem to be a complete failure in this LOVE department. I doubt I have any deep feelings about anyone, including my family. I care for my family's physical needs in super-lative form, making nutritious meals, providing a neat and clean environment, getting people to activities, and being thankful for a few minutes of quiet while I wait for the activity to finish. And my husband—oh yes, he'll be gone on business next week. That's a re-lief—one less person to plan around and want my at-tention.

But constant, gentle thought, concerned thought—no—I don't give them constant positive thought—I only put out fires.

And so it is with God. I turn to Him only when I need Him to put out fires, or when I'm so stressed I don't know where to turn. The prophet tells us that we are redeemed; we have been called by Him and are His.

It appears that God thinks of me more than I think of Him. We are told GOD IS LOVE. Ergo, He cares for me and thinks of me and my needs constantly—not just once in a while when He has nothing else to do or a thought strikes Him. "Oh yes, Suzie. I haven't thought about her for a long time. Maybe I should take a minute....Oh, there goes Saint Peter's phone. Probably another question. Maybe tomorrow."

Could we even imagine a God like this? I'm embarrassed to be this thoughtless child of His. God is LOVE—always there, always thinking about me and being concerned with my problems and needs. Do I think of Him throughout the day? At night? Last week? Occasionally? Yet He still LOVES me and calls me His own.

Thank you God for loving me. May I be as faithful to you as you are to me. May I learn to think of you constantly and be thankful that you remember me. Help me to remember that you are a part of me, and I am a part of you, that our communion with each other is what LOVE is all about.

Lynn Macmillan is a native of Milwaukee who moved to the DFW area in the mid 90s. She has been interested in the mystical and contemplative aspects of her faith for many years. She is currently a participant in a spiritual awakenings group.

You Are Worth More Than the Sparrows

Anne Marie Davis

I returned to my temporary housing after picking up my cat from *his* temporary living situation to take him to the vet. My neighbor saw me and asked how things went. I burst into tears. My sick, old cat was dehydrated and freaked out. My younger cat wouldn't come to me when I called. He just stood at the top of the stairs and cried. I had to leave them like that, scared and confused.

We'd moved to another state so my husband could work for a Christian ministry that is dear to our hearts. God had faithfully answered every prayer we had along the way. We'd moved in a hurry, which meant our new house wasn't ready for closing. We were given free temporary housing, but there was one catch: our pets couldn't live there with us. God took care of this detail, too, as a new coworker generously offered to keep our cats until we had our house. Problem solved! Or so we thought.

When I left the cats' temporary situation that day, my heart was breaking. Seeing my beloved pets so distressed, fearful, and confused hurt me deeply. They may just be animals to some people, but to us, they're family. They were miserable, and so was I. I was torn between leaving them in a home they didn't like, where I couldn't see them daily, but they had free rein, or putting them in a kennel, where I could visit often, but they'd live in a cage. Neither scenario was ideal. A tearful email went out to friends asking for prayer for what to do.

I don't know why this surprised me so much, but it did: God answered that prayer the next day in a mighty way. Our real estate agent called and said we could close on our house the very next day. We weren't due to close for another couple of weeks, but suddenly, everything moved quickly. Two days later, we owned our new house, and we had our cats back. They returned to their normal selves within two days of coming home.

This may seem a small thing in light of bigger worries in this world, but often it takes faithfulness in the little things to teach us to trust God for the big things in life. We'd seen Him answer several huge prayers regarding our move, and yet, seeing God tenderly answer a prayer for two scared little cats somehow proved His deep love for us more than the other answered prayers. If he'll rescue two small cats, how much more will He do for us? He loves us immensely. We can trust Him to take care of our needs. He's got this.

Are not two sparrows sold for a penny? Yet not one of them will fall to the ground outside your Father's care. And even the very hairs of your head are all numbered. So don't be afraid; you are worth more than many sparrows (Matthew 10:29-31).

Anne Marie Davis is a displaced Texan now living in Bartlesville, OK, with her husband, son, and two spoiled cats.

Buying That Which Is Free

Stacy Voss

*F*or the wages of sin is death, but the gift of God is eternal life through Christ Jesus our Lord (Romans 6:23).

My husband and I recently began offering our five-year-old daughter the chance to earn an allowance by keeping her room clean. Despite her excitement to receive "monies," her enthusiasm quickly diminished as she ascended the steps to tidy her room.Rather than hearing toys being thrown in their bins, the clanking of coins grew louder as she made her way to the kitchen.

"Mommy, these are for you," Micayla said, handing me thirty-one cents.

"Micayla, what is this for?"

"I want to earn my allowance," she replied, as if she could simply buy the gold star that would bring her closer to receiving a few bucks.

I had to chuckle at what seemed so preposterous, yet incredibly familiar. How many times do I attempt the same with God, trying to buy that which can't be purchased? *If only I did more, then I might merit His love*, my mind mistakenly believes. What is freely given cannot be earned.

Stacy Voss is the founder of Eyes of Your Heart Ministries (*eyesofyourheart. com*). She is known for her ability to bring biblical characters and principles to life in thought-provoking, transformative ways. She lives in Colorado with her husband and their two energetic kids.

And I pray that you, being rooted and established in love, may have power, together with all the Lord's holy people, to grasp how wide and long and high and deep is the love of Christ, and to know this love that surpasses knowledge—that you may be filled to the measure of all the fullness of God.

— Ephesians 3:17-18

God's Princesses

Denise Robinson

See what great love the Father has lavished on us, that we should be called children of God! And that is what we are! (1 John 3:1)

I loved visiting my grandparents when I was a little girl. They cancelled all of their normal activities and focused solely on our family. We would spend the week doing things that my brother and I loved doing: miniature golf, frosty mugs of root beer at the K&N, playing cards, playing dominoes and having dessert after every meal! I also loved the fact that my grandmother called me "Princess." There is no better way to start a day than hearing, "Good morning, Princess."

My own daughters loved playing "princess." They would play dress-up complete with make-shift tiaras and boas. They watched every Disney movie that involved a princess. They owned all of the "princess" Barbie dolls.

What little girl hasn't dreamed of being a princess at one time or other? And that is why I love this verse. Your heavenly Father lavishes love on you regularly. (Don't you love the word lavish? It sounds luxurious!) In fact, He lavishes you with so much love that He even calls you His child. That means that you are the daughter of the King. You are a princess! You don't have to dream anymore!

Dear Lord, Thank you for loving me so much that you call me your child. Help me to remember that all around me are also your children and they deserve to be treated that way! I love you! Amen.

Denise Robinson is the adult education director at Trietsch Memorial United Methodist Church in Flower Mound, Texas. She is passionate about the Bible and regularly leads and facilitates Bible studies.

Owe Love to Each Other

Janna Longfellow Hughes

Owe no one anything, except to love one another; for he who loves his neighbor has fulfilled the law (Romans 13:8, RSV).

At the ministry office, I played a video I'd produced for my client Chaplain Ray, a prison minister. "You turned a sow's ear into a silk purse," he said with a chuckle and a twinkle in his eye. Chaplain Ray took my hand and led me to his company comptroller's office. There he told the man to write me a check and pay me in full before I left the building.

He always did that. He took God's words seriously—*owe no man anything except to love one another.* He gave what he owed the same day. In addition to paying me, Chaplain Ray and his wife spoke words of grace and kindness.

Every time he did that, that Scripture in Romans came to mind. And being a single "mompreneur," it always helped to be paid immediately and to hear words of love.

His example also called up the apostle Paul's words:

When we are united with the Messiah Yeshua, neither being circumcised nor being uncircumcised matters; what matters is trusting faithfulness expressing itself through love (Galatians 5:6, CJB).

Chaplain Ray has gone on to his reward. His behavior stands out in my memories because no one else paid the same day the job was completed and demonstrated such care. Now I recalled his habit fondly, desiring to follow his example. Pay the debt of love we owe each other.

Our faith works by love. Do we remember our daily actions are known and read like this devotional?

Heavenly Father, help us to love each other in tangible ways today so that someone will recall what we did and know the love expressed came from you. Amen.

Janna Longfellow Hughes is a writer and television producer. She wrote the ebook *DEVELOP YOUR STORY - Tools for Building a Bridge to Your Audience*. You can find her blog at *JannaLongfellowHughes.com*.

God Calling

Mary Jane Downs

"Oh, no!" I heard my daughter shriek when I came into the den; she looked up at me with panic and said, "I've lost my cell phone in the sofa."

Sure enough it was gone into the deep recesses of the sofa where it couldn't be recovered without ripping the sofa apart. I discovered a four-inch hole in the side lining. After removing part of the bottom-lining, we were still unable to see the phone. We heard it ringing but we were unable to get to it.

In the end my daughter purchased another phone and we joked about the phone ringing in the sofa.

"Mom, your sofa is ringing. Do you want me to answer it?" It took about five days for the battery to run down.

As I was musing over this situation with a little chuckle, the Lord broke in and said, "I get treated that way from time to time."

"How so Lord?" I said.

"When you stuff me under the cushions of your life and neglect to keep the lines of communication open. Your urgency for earthly things overpowers the important spiritual necessities," He answered.

"I'm sorry Lord. Help me to be consistent with my quiet times. I know they are important to both of us. It's just that..." and I stopped myself when I realized I was beginning to make excuses for my behavior.

Is there any excuse worthy of stopping our communication with God? How do we lose the Lord in the crevices of our lives? Why can't we hear Him calling for us to come away for a moment of rest and wisdom?

Many people spend a lot of time and effort searching for people who will understand them. God is freely available at any time of the day or night when we call upon His name and open our hearts to receive His word. All we need is faith to begin a lifetime of love in the Father's presence. He understands you perfectly and loves you eternally.

Remember: *Indeed, the very hairs of your head are all numbered. Don't be afraid; you are worth more than many sparrows* (Luke 12:7).

Are you ready to regularly "schedule" Christ into your life? Jesus will quietly ask but He will not nag or beg you for time. You have to come out of your own free will. If you have been off balance lately, now is a great time to reconnect. Christ is waiting for you with open arms and a heart of love saying, "Come."

Mary Jane Downs is a writer and blogger from the foothills of Asheville, North Carolina. Her blog *Joy in the Morning,* can be found at *maryjanewrites.com.*

Intentional Love

Lisa Burkhardt Worley

I love birthday celebrations! Over the weekend we celebrated a close friend's 50th at a beautiful high tea and lunch. I admire this friend a great deal because she extends God's love to everyone she meets.

While most people are in a hurry nowadays and don't have time to connect, she is intentional about reaching out to people and takes time to get to know them. She realizes that she is not a "group" person and likes focusing on people one-on-one. She loves others as she loves herself.

On Friday, a woman with a disfiguring skin disease attended our monthly women's luncheon. I was so happy she decided to come, and I greeted her warmly, as did others. Later, I talked to my friend about her and she told me, "I gave her my phone number and told her that if she ever needed to talk to someone, that she should call me." I was ashamed! Why didn't I reach out in that way? But that is the kind of person my friend is.

While Jesus spoke to the crowds, He was also intentional about His love and focused on people individually. One of the best examples I can think of is in Luke 19. Jesus is being followed by throngs of people when He spots tax collector, Zacchaeus, perched in a tree. At that point, the crowd is airbrushed out and all that exists in the world are Jesus and Zacchaeus, when Jesus offers His hand of friendship. He looks up with a smile and says, *Zacchaeus, come down immediately. I must stay at your house today* (Luke 19:5).

Zacchaeus didn't know Jesus before, but Jesus made a point to know him, and through His love, brought Zacchaeus out of the tree. Zacchaeus must have felt Jesus' warmth radiating towards him while he sat in the branches. That was all it took. Zacchaeus was now a believer!

When you are out in the world, do you look for that person you can call down from the tree? How often are you intentional about your love? I know that I personally have a tendency to move so fast that I don't always see the tree dwellers, but I desire to be more like Jesus, don't you? *Lord, please help us to slow down and show us who needs our intentional love today!*

Lisa Burkhardt Worley is a former national television sports reporter, now Christian motivational speaker and writer and is the founder of Pearls of Promise Ministries, *pearlsofpromiseministries.com*. She is the co-author of the award winning manuscript, *If I Only Had...Following God's Path to Your Security*. "Like" POP on Facebook at */pearlsofpromiseministries*.

Walking With My Abba

Lisa Mick

The other day I took my usual walk down a wood trail by my house. I love this walk because God always brings the usual creatures out for me to admire: squirrels scamper and birds chirp their sweet songs. Most walks I get to pet a dog or two.

This walk was different though because I knew the Lord journeyed with me. My relationship with Abba, my father, has grown over the past few years so we spend more time with each other during the day now.

Strolling down the path, I said to my Father, "If I am really hearing you, feeling you, and sensing your presence with me, please show me a sign." All of a sudden, three squirrels started at the bottom of three different trees and scampered up to the same spot and started chattering. The squirrels stopped at the same height and turned and looked at me while they were communicating.

Most of the time when I see squirrels, there are only two speaking to each other and they aren't looking at me. This time I realized God's holy presence was there with me on that bridge. The trio of squirrels, connecting with me, swishing their precious tails, answered a question that I had been wondering about. Since I've drawn closer to the Lord, I feel His Presence in the most unusual way as tiny electrical currents start at my feet and run through my entire body. During my moment with the squirrels, the currents were flowing!

Oh how marvelous is this new added presence of Him to my life! The Father had answered me completely. I have fellowship with Him because I walk in His ways.

Sisters, you can have a similar experience if you spend time with our Father, walking with Him, communicating while you are driving around town on your many errands or speaking with Him while you are in your homes. He is waiting on you to be in HIS presence. The more time you spend with Him the closer He will be.

James 4:8 says, *Come near to God and He will come near to you.* Will you ask your Father to take a walk with you today?

Lisa Mick is the director of outreach for Pearls of Promise Ministries and is also one of the editors for the *Pearls of Promise* devotional. Lisa is also co-authoring a Bible study designed to help non-writers record their faith journey. She is a regular contributor to the Pearls of Promise blog at *pearlsofpromiseministries.com.*

Pearls of Joy

Breakfast Blessings

LeAnn Weiss-Rupard

I'll never forget one year in junior high when my mom made an extra effort to make us hot breakfasts like French toast. Mom wanted to teach us about the wonders of God and His personal involvement in the lives of His children. Starting in Exodus, she read from the Bible to us for ten minutes each morning as we ate.

Mom challenged us, "As I read, look for all the good things that God did for the children of Israel." This became a fun daily game. We talked about miracles, such as when God sent plagues to free the Israelites from Egypt or parted the Red Sea. But we also discussed God's little blessings, like the manna He provided every day.

Another part of our game was identifying all the times God's chosen people complained. I quickly noticed a pattern... God gave great blessings, but then the Israelites developed selective amnesia and grumbled. Instead of focusing on their blessings, they focused on what they didn't have.

Mom noted, "When life is good, it's easy to get prideful and to forget God. 1 Samuel 12:34 teaches us to think about the good things God has done for us."

Next, Mom helped us make a blessing basket. She cut strips of colored paper and asked us to write our names and something good God had done in our lives. We'd add new items of gratefulness to the basket throughout the week. Then, we'd frequently pull a strip from the basket and thank God.

To this day, those devotions still have a major impact

148

on my joy factor. I've learned to realize that when I have an attitude of gratitude toward God, nothing can steal my joy. But when the enemy gets me to focus on my wants, it's a slippery slope that quickly sabotages my joy by luring me into the comparison and entitlement trap. Then I'm a malcontent and ingrate myself.

I've had the privilege to travel around the world including several trips to Africa and Europe as well as visiting Guatemala and Brazil. Our blessings in the U.S. are so huge compared to most of the world. And yet I've observed more complaining here than some of the poorest countries.

In 1996, I chaperoned a group of teens from my church on a mission trip to Guatemala. We slept on the dirt floors of humble huts. There wasn't any plumbing or running water. Those villagers sacrificed their meals for days just to be able to feed us. They had virtually nothing and yet they exhibited sheer joy in sharing what little they had.

I love what Tommy Newberry says in *40 Days to a Joy-Filled Life*: "When you are right with God, you humbly cherish life for what it is: a temporary gift, a treasure with an unknown expiration date. This connection with God naturally breeds awe of life, thankfulness for what life has to offer, and gratitude for what you can offer the world with His help."

LeAnn Weiss-Rupard is a gifted encourager. Her joy comes from helping to inspire writers, leaders, and ministries around the world. She founded Encouragement Company in 1994 where she strives to build up other encouragers. LeAnn can be reached at *ECblessing@cs.com* or on Facebook under LeAnn Weiss-Rupard. She resides in Granbury, TX with her husband Rick.

Dryer Vent Pumpkins

Lisa Burkhardt Worley

Every year our church holds a craft fair called "Fall on the Mound." Vendors from all over North Texas come to sell their artistic creations with the proceeds from the booth rental fee going towards women's ministry activities and missions.

As I was walking around all the booths, I spotted an unusual, yet beautiful array of bright orange pumpkins displayed by a women's group from our church. As I admired them, the pumpkin artist chirped, "They're made out of dryer vents!" I thought, "How could something so cute be handcrafted from something so ordinary?"

It occurred to me that Christ does the same with our lives! 2 Corinthians 5:17 assures us, *Therefore, if anyone is in Christ, he is a new creation; the old has gone, the new has come!* God loves to take the ordinary and transform it into the extraordinary! I bought a trio of dryer vent pumpkins to serve as a reminder of Jesus' transforming power.

I remember hearing a story in seminary about St. Augustine that I have never forgotten. Before his conversion, St. Augustine was involved in loose living that involved drinking and many women. After he committed to Christ, a woman from his past was trying to get his attention as he walked down the road. He didn't answer her calls. She finally caught up to him and said something like, "Augustine, why didn't you turn around when I called you?" He replied, "Young woman, I am not that man anymore."

And so it is with us. When we give our lives to Christ, we are no longer the same person. God takes a life headed for the dumpster and creates a treasure—YOU—to be used for His glory. The problem is sometimes we still see ourselves as junk rather than a piece of art. We must claim the truth about our new life in Christ and realize God is molding us into something very special.

The next time you doubt your value to God, make yourself a promise to remember the dryer vent pumpkins; and know that God has blown new life into you!

Lisa Burkhardt Worley, is a former national television sports reporter, now Christian motivational speaker and writer, and is the founder of Pearls of Promise Ministries, *pearlsofpromiseministries.com*. She is the co-author of the award winning manuscript, *If I Only Had...Following God's Path to Your Security*, is an editor for the *Pearls of Promise* devotional and has a Masters of Theological Studies Degree from Perkins School of Theology.

God's Gifts and Blessings

Lisa Mick

My husband, Dennis, and I recently traveled for two weeks for his work. As we were on the road going from Texas to Florida we passed a sign to Dothan, Alabama.

"Honey, I think this is where my grandfather was born. I think my family cemetery is there," I said. So when we reached our destination that evening, he looked on his computer and found *findagrave.com*. Someone had posted a picture of the headstones that were in the cemetery in Dothan. Wow. We were amazed. We found my great-great grandfather and my great-great-great grandparent's headstones. I knew I would have to see this one day.

Almost two weeks later, on our way home from our trip, Dennis asked me if I wanted to take a side-trip to see the cemetery where my family members rested. "Can we please?" It was way out in the country in Alabama and with the help of technology and the latitude and longitude, my precious husband located our family plots.

What a blessing I received standing in the Granberry Cemetery which was started with my great-great-great grandfather in 1858. God placed my ancestors amongst big trees and on a hill surrounded by cotton. Snow white cotton surrounded the cemetery making it feel like we were in the clouds. It was beautiful and peaceful.

Back on the road, hours into the trip, I was struck by one regret: I didn't get any cotton to remind me of our visit. I looked over at Dennis and told him I wanted to cry because I forgot to pick some cotton as a remembrance. Dennis looked over at me with a big smile as he pulled some cotton out of his shirt pocket.

"I got it for you, Honey, and was going to surprise you with it."

My sweet Father had not only led us to that cemetery but He used His gift to me, my husband, to give me a blessing. He knew I would want a keepsake but would forget it in all the excitement. To see Dennis' face and to know how much he wanted to give me that gift also was about more than I could take that day!

God is always looking to bless us and give us His precious gifts. *All these blessings will come upon you and accompany you if you obey the LORD your God* (Deuteronomy 28:2). Sometimes His blessings are right under our nose, sometimes they are right beside us and other times God uses those around us to bring us special gifts. I am very thankful I have God to guide my days and my husband to share them with me.

If you, then, though you are evil, know how to give good gifts to your children, how much more will your Father in heaven give good gifts to those who ask Him! (Matthew 7:11)

Lisa Mick is director of outreach for Pearls of Promise Ministries and is also one of the editors for the *Pearls of Promise* devotional. Lisa is also co-authoring a Bible study that helps non-writers to record their faith journey. She is a regular contributor to the Pearls of Promise blog at *pearlsofpromiseministries.com.*

Getting Lost

Lisa Burkhardt Worley

On our 25th anniversary trip to Puerto Rico, one of my favorite days was a result of being lost. On our first full day in Puerto Rico, we were trying to find a bakery, but ended up past our intended destination in a community called Naguabo. At Naguabo, we discovered not only a beautiful area to look at, but we also found a wonderful restaurant overlooking the water and decided to stop in for lunch.

While seated on the balcony of the restaurant, an older gentleman, standing below, signaled for our attention and asked if we'd be interested in snorkeling in the bay at Naguabo. Talk about direct marketing! I had tried to set up a snorkeling trip for us before leaving for Puerto Rico, but it had not worked out. This seemed to be a perfect opportunity, so after looking at his marketing material stashed in his car, we scheduled our snorkeling trip with Captain Paco Lopez for three days later, on Thursday.

Captain Paco turned out to be quite a character, entertaining us with his outgoing personality and at times, serenading us with a musical instrument made out of a sea shell. Every time Captain Paco passed another boat or someone on the shore near us, He made Himself known by blowing into the mouth of the sea-shell, which sounded a lot like a foghorn.

Captain Paco was not only informative about the area, but also had an amazingly positive outlook on life, despite a bout with melanoma cancer that he told us about while on our snorkeling tour. In Captain

Paco's eyes, life could not be better than right there on the water in Naguabo.

As I reflected on the day, I thought, "We would have never had this delightful excursion if we had not gotten lost." I also thought, "But God knew where He was taking us." Proverbs 16:9 says, *In their hearts humans plan their course, but the LORD establishes their steps.* We had a plan that first day in Puerto Rico, but the Lord directed our steps to a much more enjoyable destination.

If only we could get lost in the Lord more often.... I wonder where He would take us?

Lisa Burkhardt Worley is a former national television sports reporter, now Christian motivational speaker and writer and is the founder of Pearls of Promise Ministries, *pearlsofpromiseministries.com*. She is the co-author of the award winning manuscript, *If I Only Had...Following God's Path to Your Security*, and is an editor for the *Pearls of Promise* devotional.

Rejoice!

Caroline Gavin

Rejoice in the Lord always. I will say it again: Rejoice! (Philippians 4:4)

The trees rejoice in red,
The sky sings in blue,
Indeed all of the earth
Seems to sing of You.

Leaves dance in the wind,
Rivers flow ever free,
Surely it is for You
This joyful dance I see.

A caress from a breeze,
A kiss from a raindrop,
From the deep valley
To the towering mountaintop—

Yes, all of the world
Joins in the celebration;
For our Lord, our Creator,
Sings all of creation.

Our deep joy in You
How can we restrain?
You are sweet symphony,
Our melodic refrain.

Indeed my very heart
For You does beat;
It sings of You, Jesus,
Of Your love ever sweet.

With the rivers and mountains,
With the trees and sky,
I rejoice in my Savior,
My God, the Most High.

We are nothing at all
Without our Lord, our King;
It is no wonder then
Our hearts forever sing.

Yea, my heart wells with joy,
Nature joins me in song:
Rejoice, rejoice,
For with Jesus we belong.

From the deep valley
To the towering mountaintop,
From the crisp breeze,
To the gentle raindrop—

In all, sweet Jesus,
Your eternal love I see;
I dance in Your presence,
You set my spirit free.

So as trees rejoice in red,
As the sky sings in blue,
I join all of the earth
To sing this song of You.

Caroline Gavin is a Christian life coach, speaker, author and host of Purposeful Pathway Radio. She is committed to helping others find their paths, live with purpose, and walk God's way. Refresh with her poetry at *PurposefulPathway.com* and in the forty-day poetic devotional book *Purposeful Pathway: Your Journey with Jesus.*

The Focus on Joy

Karen Ambler

Fifty-eight years. Fifty-eight years of marriage, and here she stood, over her dear husband's hospital bed, praying for a miracle. That's where Bendito and I met George and Ginger while making our rounds as a dog therapy team.

They happily welcomed us into the dimly lit room and to George's bedside. He was propped up, a pile of pillows behind his head, and wearing huge, dark sunglasses over bandaged eyes, and though they were quite obtrusive, they were barely noticeable above his beaming smile which had a light all its own. His hands, with skin like fragile parchment, reached out to touch Bendito. His sweet bride began to patiently describe in great detail my tiny long-haired Chihuahua: the large furry ears, one up, one down...the white feet with black spots...his long fluffy white-tipped tail...on she went making sure George could picture his little four-footed visitor clearly in his mind. This may read like a pathetic, pitiable scene, and may have been, if it were not for one outstanding and undeniable emotion that pervaded that little hospital room: Joy.

While Bendito snuggled into George's lap, Ginger began to describe to me the extremely rare disease that was stealing her husband's precious vision. So rare, in fact, that they had to travel thousands of miles to a specialist to get an accurate diagnosis. Treatment goes on for years, with a myriad of unpleasant side effects, and is often unsuccessful. The tone with which she described their inconceivable ordeal, though, was not unlike one a person would use to tell of the inconvenience of a flat tire, or the disappointment of a cancelled appointment. Not that it was trivial to them, but so sure was she that their God was in control this unexpected detour in their lives was simply part of God's good plan for them. They knew and trusted the One who made the plan for them. And joy reigned in their hearts. *For I know the plans I have for you, declares the LORD, plans to prosper you and not to harm you, plans to give you hope and a future* (Jeremiah 29:11).

Little Bendito was fast asleep now, lulled off to sweet dreams by this dear man's gentle, loving touch. He slept on through Ginger's chatty exuberance as she told me of their large family—six children, eighteen grandchildren, eleven great-grandchildren and two more on the way. She nearly bubbled over recounting their penchant for Polka dancing and how they had traveled the country to various Polka events throughout their lives. George quipped that he was still a pretty good dancer, but people better best get out of his way since he can't see where he's going! We laughed. A lot. How thankful they were, too, for their loving church family. Our uplifting visit continued as the vast majority of our time was spent with their testifying of the many blessings God had bestowed upon them. Without question that is where their focus lay—on God's gifts. And joy poured from their hearts. *The LORD has done great things for us, and we are filled with joy* (Psalm 126:3).

Nurses came in to see to George's treatment. I gathered my sleepy "therapist" into my arms to make my departure, but not before promising to pray for healing, and making an unspoken promise to myself to learn from their example to choose joy in all circumstances. *Though the fig tree does not bud and there are no grapes on the vines, though the olive crop fails and the fields produce no food, though there are no sheep in the pen and no cattle in the stalls, yet I will rejoice in the* LORD, *I will be joyful in God my Savior* (Habakkuk 3:17-18).

Karen Ambler's passion is helping women discover their true identity in Christ and find freedom through His Word. Karen mentors and leads Bible studies through her home-based ministry "For The Joy." She also ministers to hurting people with her registered therapy dog, Bendito, through Blessed Be Animal Assisted Therapy. Contact Karen at *blessedbeforthejoy.com.*

But let all who take refuge in you be glad; let them ever sing for joy.

Spread your protection over them, that those who love your name may rejoice in you.

— Psalm 5:11

Leaves, Wind and Beauty

Cathy Biggerstaff

Leaves raining
on the landscape below
and the wind whistling
her bone-chilling song,
leave barren sticks in the place
where breath-taking beauty had been,
just a day or two ago.

Reds and yellows,
oranges and browns,
Any florist would proudly claim
the arrangement of brilliant colors
in the hillside display.
sweeps fall away into winter.

Thank you, Lord,
for this one last blast of dazzling color
I can hold in my heart,
until winter throws off his dull, gray coat
and spring bursts forth again.

Cathy Biggerstaff blogs weekly at *cathybiggerstaff.blogspot.com*. She writes children's books and curriculum, as well as devotional materials. Cathy is published in *Mature Living Magazine*, on *ChristianDevotions.us*, and she guest blogs. She leads the Encouragers Christian Writers Group. Cathy is a Christian Clown and uses this avenue to reach people with the Gospel. Contact her at *hiskid410@gmail.com*.

Those the LORD
has rescued will
return. They will enter
Zion with singing;
everlasting joy will
crown their heads.

Gladness and joy will
overtake them, and
sorrow and sighing
will flee away.

— Isaiah 51:11

An Oasis in the Desert

Stephanie Shott

Your love has given me great joy and encouragement, because you, brother, have refreshed the hearts of the saints (Philemon 1:7).

When I was a little girl, we took a trip to California and our drive led us through the dry Nevada desert. I remember how sweltering hot it was during the day and how freezing cold it became at night. Our car didn't have any air conditioning or heat, so we felt the extremes of both.

The road was long and barren. No restaurants, no gas stations, no hotels, no Zippy Marts. Nothing. Just a dry desert. Then all of a sudden, in the hazy distance, we spotted what appeared to be a gas station. In the middle of nowhere, it stood out like an oasis and we couldn't wait to get there.

We pulled into the seemingly abandoned building and waited to see if there was anyone there. An old man flung the door open wide, welcomed us and began pumping our gas, cleaning our windshields and talking a mile a minute.

As we made our way up the steps of the building and started to open the door, the cold air seemed to blast through the doorway bringing smiles to our faces. We loitered there for about thirty minutes, buying peanut brittle and bubble gum and looking for anything else we could find to extend our time at that little oasis in the middle of nowhere.

We said good-bye to the nice man who had invited us into his world and allowed his gas station to become a temporary refuge for our little family. We left refreshed and ready to make the last leg of our trip, thankful for that oasis in the desert.

We all need an oasis of encouragement from time to time. A place where we can go...a refuge where our hearts long to linger and be refreshed.

Every day, we have the opportunity to invite others into our world, to speak life into someone else's life, to be an oasis in the desert places of their lives, to be a blast of cool air in the hot, dry circumstances of someone's world.

Today, ask the Lord to give you an opportunity to refresh someone's soul, to help someone in need.

Come to me, all who labor and are heavy laden, and I will give you rest (Matthew 11:28).

Stephanie Shott is an author, speaker and ministry leader who leads women to live full, fearless and faithful lives. Founder of: The M.O.M. Initiative, a missional mentoring ministry devoted to taking Titus 2 to the streets. You can find out more about The M.O.M. Initiative by visiting *themominitiative. com*. Stephanie's website is *stephanieshott.com*.

Choosing Joy

Lisa Mick

*Y*ou will make known to me the path of life; you will fill me with joy in your presence, with eternal pleasures at your right hand (Psalm 16:11).

Living one's life in the past is defeating but I did this for years. Although my life was full of good and bad, the negative seemed to always be alive in my mind. Have you ever replayed your life choices over and over again? Even after you have asked forgiveness from your Father and know you are forgiven?

For me, the negative was etched in my mind. What needed to transpire was a change from negative to positive thinking. Some sweet person led me to see I was letting this hinder my life in such a way that JOY was not evident in my walk. Wow! Could someone really see those secret negative places? Do our lives reveal what lies in our mind and soul? You bet they do. That day caused a switch to go off. I started reading and searching about negative patterns that people let themselves fall into. As it turned out, I was reading about myself.

I have known our sweet Heavenly Father almost all of my life but didn't really walk with Him until a short time ago. The scripture above states *you will fill me with joy in your presence*. What does that really mean? Well, I started a gratitude journal of everyday blessings. Slowly my thought process began to change. God's Word and gratitude brought JOY.

A dear friend said to me, "Just choose joy." I now understand what she meant. Realizing that I can't find joy on my own, I needed to walk with our Heavenly Father hour by hour, day by day and converse with Him constantly. Choosing joy means spending time with our Father and letting Him *make known to you the path of life*. It means studying His Word, applying it in your daily life and most importantly spending time in prayer with Him. This in turn fills you up with JOY.

Choose joy today in your life; it has made a huge difference in my life and others see it. We are to be witnesses and shine His light. I pray He shines thru you as well dear friend. Make the choice to follow Christ and with Him you will find JOY.

Lisa Mick is director of outreach for Pearls of Promise Ministries and is also one of the editors for the *Pearls of Promise* devotional. Lisa is also co-authoring a Bible study that helps non-writers record their faith journey. She is a regular contributor to the Pearls of Promise blog at *pearlsofpromiseministries.com*. Email Lisa at *lisamick@pearlsofpromiseministries.com*.

A Tale of the Not Quite So Good Samaritan

Lynn Macmillan

A man was going down from Jerusalem to Jericho, when he was attacked by robbers. They stripped him of his clothes, beat him and went away, leaving him half dead... But a Samaritan, as he traveled, came where the man was; ... He went to him and bandaged his wounds, pouring on oil and wine. Then he put the man on his own donkey, brought him to an inn and took care of him (Luke 10:30-35).

One day, I was walking near the river, enjoying a spring day, anticipating a quiet lunch break from a hectic workday with a thankful pleasurable sigh. Many others had the same idea because there were no empty park benches and I realized I was going to have to either share a bench or go somewhere else. I chose plan A which meant sharing the bench. I sat down and started unpacking my lunch—sandwich, chips, V-8, and the best looking plum I'd had in quite a while. Sitting at the other end of the bench was someone I didn't recognize as homeless until I had settled myself.

I unwrapped my lunch and started on my sandwich. I was into the 2nd half of the sandwich when I began to feel more than a little uncomfortable. It's hard to enjoy your lunch when you know the person sitting a few feet away probably wouldn't have any lunch at all. I looked at my lovely plum (which was all that was left without bite marks) and my heart felt a warm kindness toward the young man.

I held out the plum and asked if he would like it. He slowly took it from me and carefully looked it over. Then, in a motion that would have made any professional pitcher proud, he took the plum and threw it into the river. I was speechless as he slowly got up and walked away. My beautiful plum I had ripened for a week—having reached perfection—was now food for carp at the bottom of the dirty, polluted river.

I thought about my "selfless" act of charity. What had I expected from the young man—gushing gratitude? Certainly not the reaction I got. He probably never gave the plum incident another thought but I have. If I had known what he was going to do with my perfect plum, would I have still given it to him? Probably not. That doesn't say much for my charitable acts. I guess I wanted acknowledgment of this "great" thing I'd done.

But, to be kinder to myself, I often think of that young man and his rejection of my gift. Would I do that same thing today? Yes, I think I would. Why? Because the act, so rudely rejected, reminds me of the rejections Jesus faced. Then I feel the warmth of Christ's love as He says: "well done" my faithful servant. There is no greater joy that could be wished for than Jesus' approval of a lesson of quiet giving and rejection, well learned.

Lynn Macmillan is a native of Milwaukee who moved to the DFW area in the mid 90s. She has been interested in the mystical and contemplative aspects of her faith for many years. She is currently a participant in a Spiritual Awakenings group.

Pearls of
Peace

Claustrophobic Panic or His Peace

Catherine Weiskopf

*D*o not be anxious about anything, but in every situation, by prayer and petition, with thanksgiving, present your requests to God. And the peace of God, which transcends all understanding, will guard your hearts and your minds in Christ Jesus (Philippians 4: 6-7).

As the jet roared down the runway, I gripped the blue vinyl armrest of my airplane seat and struggled to control my breathing. When the airplane prepared to soar, my panic attack did the same. Feelings of being trapped overwhelmed my shaking body. For the next two hours, I fought the hand-sweating, mind-electrifying panic second-by-second. At the end of the flight, I walked down the hangar feeling limp, depressed, and exhausted. I wondered how I could survive a flight again?

A year later, as soon as I booked the same flight home, I dreaded it. I felt incapable of handling the mental pressure without cracking. The problem was, I could keep the panic at bay for a few minutes, but the flight was two and one-half hours long. If only I could focus on God the whole time. After all, God says, "fear not." Praying brought me peace, but panic constantly wormed its way into my mind and destroyed my peace.

The night before we left, amongst all the worry, in the middle of imagining the worst airplane flight ever, I desperately prayed for help. God then focused a spotlight on my delirious thinking. My anxiety came because I didn't think I could focus on God. It was still all about me and my strength, my focus, my ability. God told me to rely on Him for my food, my children's well-being, and yes even my faith and my ability to concentrate on Him. "Yes, Dear God, keep my mind on you. You know I can't do it, but you can."

I'd like to say after I prayed all the fear evaporated instantly, but even Abraham had to wait for his prayer for children to be answered. Flight day, the anticipation was miserable. I walked down the tin can tunnels, through the doors, past seat after seat of people packed in like sardines. Would God come through for me? I quickly said a prayer that mimicked the father who brought his demon possessed son to Jesus, *I do believe; help me overcome my unbelief* (Mark 9:24). We taxied to our takeoff; the engine roared; we raced down the track. The airplane lifted and the wheels pulled up.

Where were the closed in feelings, the panic? They had vanished. In their place, for the whole two and one-half hours, God kept me in perfect peace.

That day God taught me to rely on Him for everything, even my faith in Him. And that day, God replaced my armrest-gripping, claustrophobic panic with His dependable glorious peace.

Dear God, help me to rely on You for everything, even my faith and focus.

Catherine Weiskopf is the creative director of POP Ministries. She is a Christian and educational writer dedicated to helping others tell their stories. She is the co-author of the award winning manuscript, *If I Only Had... Following God's Path to Your Security*, and is currently co-authoring two Bible studies. Contact her at *cweiskopf@pearlsofpromiseministries.com*.

God's Peace for Parents

Beth Shriver

Train up a child in the way he should go and when he is old he will not depart from it (Proverbs 22:6, KJV).

I've written a number of fiction books, but the one non-fiction book I wrote was harder to write than any of them. Our move to Texas was difficult, especially for my daughter. Her first year in high school was so challenging we decided to move her to a private Christian school.

I'd lie in bed and fret over things I had no control over. I had a stack of devotionals on my bedside table, but none of them quite fit what we were going through. So, I began writing my own. I continued writing them off-and-on for years. It takes me less than a year to write a fiction book but this was non-fiction, something new for me, and it was personal, not fictional characters in a make-believe world that I could control.

Every time my girl fell into trouble I'd write a devotional, when she was doing okay I'd stop and go back to my fiction. Both gave me strength in different ways.

Four years later when I was submitting a fiction manuscript to my agent she asked, "This is a great story, but when are you going to finish those devotionals?" My answer, "I'll be done with them when my daughter's done."

When I got the final galleys for the devotional and saw the formatting I was thrilled. Each page flowed beautifully and was easy on the eyes. But that wasn't the only reason for my joy, my girl was done. She was in college, living in her own apartment, working and doing much better.

When I signed the contract, I remembered feeling a bit scared and exposed. A part of us would be out there for hundreds of people to read about. But then a sense of peace flowed over me thinking...but I need to share this because I wish I would have had these devotionals when I needed them. It was then I heard God's voice say, "You did. You wrote them."

Faith Step: Parenting teens can be hard, so will you make the effort to help others, and ask for help when you need it?

Beth Shriver is the author of three books, *Annie's Truth, Grace Given,* and *Healing Grace.* You can find her at *BethShriverWriter.com.*

God's Lesson Plan

Karen Ferrell

I'm a list maker and a planner. I like to be prepared. So I worry. About things I can control, like what to fix for dinner. And about things totally beyond my control: the weather, my son's life choices, the state of the nation... Well, you get the idea.

"Let go and let God" has never been easy advice for me to follow.

High on my all-planned-out list was my career. I was an educator, but also dreamed of being a full-time writer. So I worked in an "in between" administrative position and pursued the dream during tiny slots of spare time.

A few years before my retirement, budgets got slashed and so did my administrative position. Fortunately, I still had a job, but not the one I'd planned on. I was reassigned mid-year as a high school geometry teacher. I'd taught middle school math, but never high school anything. Because of my predecessor's poor health and absences, the students were behind in their studies. For that matter, when it came to high school geometry, so was I.

In Jeremiah 29:11 God assures us, *For I know the plans I have for you...plans to give you a future and a hope.*

Confronted by a room full of students being force-fed a daily dose of geometry, I couldn't imagine how this could possibly be part of His plan for me.

But slowly, God's blessings piled up. On my first day a boy said, "I learned more today than I have all year." Another student proudly displayed his pop quiz grade. "That's the highest grade I've gotten in this class." A vice-principal congratulated me on the lack of disciplinary referrals. I received a thank-you note from a parent for helping her daughter succeed in math for the first time in her educational life.

At the end of year, the principal asked if I planned to return next year. His question surprised me. I hadn't even considered leaving. Suddenly, I realized why. I was happier in the classroom than in administration. I enjoyed the challenge of translating math terms into plain English and seeing those "ah ha" moments that lit up a student's eyes. I loved the classroom. It was where I belonged. And God had put me there.

When I retired from education, it was as a high school geometry teacher. But God had also used my classroom experience to help me fulfill my dream. I was also a published author. The topic of my books: Math. Without my secondary math classroom experience, I'd never been qualified to write them.

Looking back at my initial fear and anxiety, I'm reminded of the saying "Agree with me now. It will save so much time."

God said it better in Job 22:21: *Agree with God, and be at peace; thereby good will come to you* (ESV).

Dear God, Help me to let go of my own plans, to trust your judgment, and to turn my tomorrows over to you. Amen.

Karen Ferrell is the author of *Adventures in Mathopolis, GameWize* and *Partnering Microsoft Excel with Math.* Her website is *karenferrell.net.*

I See You

Martha Helton

She gave this name to the LORD who spoke to her: You are the God who sees me, for she said, I have now seen the One who sees me (Genesis 16:13).

When my son, Tyler, was about six months old, I had a favorite game I would play with him. As I drove, I would look into the rearview mirror, catch his gaze, and say, "I see you!" He would erupt into giggles. No matter how many times my new-mom infatuation propelled me to look in the mirror, he would squeal in delight.

In God's mirror, the Bible, we see Hagar, a young Egyptian slave who belonged to Sarai. Because Sarai grew tired of waiting on God's promise for her and Abram to have children, her solution was to give Hagar to her husband as his wife. Abram passively agreed. Hagar conceived, but jealousy grew between Hagar and Sarai and the cat-fight ensued. Once again, passive Abram pushed the matter onto Sarai after she sought his intervention. Sarai, in turn, so mistreated Hagar that she fled into the desert.

Poor Hagar had no choice about her station in life as a slave. She felt forgotten, unnoticed and misunderstood. She certainly wasn't feeling the love from Sarai or protection from her so-called husband, Abram. Despair drove her into the scorching desert, pregnant and without much food or water. But wait...there was someone there who saw her in her anguish. An angel of the Lord appeared to her and asked, "Hagar, slave of Sarai, where have you come from, and where are you going?"

"I'm running away from my mistress Sarai," she answered.

Then the angel of the LORD told her, "Go back to your mistress and submit to her." The angel added, "I will increase your descendants so much that they will be too numerous to count...you will give birth to a son. You shall name him Ishmael, for the LORD has heard of your misery."

Hagar's response? "You are the God who sees me," for she said, "I have now seen the One who sees me." So touched by this supernatural encounter, Hagar called the well where this interchange took place, Beer Lahai Roi—which means "well of the Living One who sees me."

Isn't that true for us? When we feel understood and loved, we "see" each other. In the James Cameron film, *Avatar* Jake Sully and Neytiri share a poignant scene where she sees him in his true human form, yet lovingly looks into his eyes and softly says, "I see you."

"I see you," he tenderly responds. Spiritually speaking, we can lovingly lock eyes with our heavenly Daddy, knowing He not only sees us physically, but also sees our true, human form, inside and out. "I see you," God says as He's gazing in the mirror at you, eyes twinkling. Now *that* is something to squeal about!

Martha Helton is a stay-at-home wife to her sweet husband and mother to three awesome sons who do freelancing and proofing for small town magazines. She is an avid trash-to-treasure collector who is gathering tidbits of truth from her life to write a book revealing how God has shaped and is shaping her junk into surprisingly, beautiful gems. Contact her at *marthahelton@gmail.com*.

Just Breathe

Macey Hart

I don't breathe easy like most people. Diagnosed with asthma, I have 50% lung capacity unless I use my rescue inhaler which brings me up to a mere 75%. To combat this problem, my pulmonary doctor prescribed pulmonary rehabilitation. This meant going to the hospital twice a week for four to six weeks and meeting with a pulmonary therapist. The doctors found that somehow through life, I'd slowly stopped breathing correctly through the stress of "winter seasons"(or unhappy times). This past year, with the grief and sorrow of losing my mother and daddy, my breathing got worse.

God also revealed to me that my neck muscle tension was caused by using my neck and chest muscles to breathe instead of my diaphragm! My prescription from the doctor was to relearn how to breathe right and to attempt to increase my lung capacity.

In addition to the doctor prescription I also received instructions from the Great Physician. Over the course of a few months I had been praying for God to heal me so I could have more energy.

In answer to my prayers, God sent me to a Bible study on contentment. He wanted to teach me that I should never let the unhappy times in life get me so down that I stop breathing correctly! He wanted me to learn how to be content in every season of life. Even in the stressful winters of life, I need to "just breathe" so that I would not adversely affect my health. Many anxious people hold their breath. They are not even aware they do this. This is an unconscious reaction to anxiety. If you have this problem, learn to become conscious of this tendency to hold your breath. Each time this is discovered, release your breath slowly and practice slow, abdominal breathing, at least for a breath or two to break the cycle of anxiety controlling your breath.

God's word tells us in Philippians 4:6-7: *Do not be anxious about anything, but in every situation, by prayer and petition, with thanksgiving, present your requests to God. And the peace of God, which transcends all understanding, will guard your hearts and your minds in Christ Jesus.*

In addition to our own efforts to improve our breathing, it is important to turn our breathing over to God. God is the one who determines how many breaths we will take in this life, so He enables us to breathe easier if we give our worries to Him. God wants us to give our worries to Him and "Just Breathe!"

Macey Hart is a professional photographer in Flower Mound, Texas and owns Macey Hart Photography. She donates her time and talents to Pearls of Promise Ministries. You can find her at *maceyhartphotography.com.*

Rescued

Jennifer Mersberger

My family has grown by four feet. After months of researching dog breeds and looking into several sad little puppy eyes, we finally adopted a little dog from a local shelter. She's a Beagle/Chihuahua mix (or as we like to say, a be-huahua) named Chica.

The first night in our home, Chica lay sleeping on my lap. I wondered what kind of stories she would tell me if she could. What had she been through and how did she end up living in a cage?

Was she rejected? Pushed aside, or even sent away because someone thought she was lacking?

Was she still afraid? Does fear cause her to cower down or lash out? What scares her most?

How long was she alone? I'm not sure which is worse, being afraid of those around you or being completely on your own?

I guess when it comes down to it, we're all like Chica. We need to be rescued. We need to know that our perception doesn't have to be our reality. Our situation can change and we can be made better by it. We weren't meant to live in a cage, we were meant to live our lives to the full.

Our Rescuer, Father God, longs to set every last one of us free. He wants to release us from the bars that hold us and replace our fears and doubts with His love and strength. He invites us to rest in Him as He protects us from our enemies.

We are chosen. God calls us each by name, longing to give us an eternal home.

We are victorious. In the battle of good versus evil, God has won! Through Him, we cannot be defeated.

We are loved. God loves us so much that He gives us His Holy Spirit so we will never be alone.

We welcomed Chica into our family, hoping to share a lifetime of joy with her. God welcomes us into His family to share in His joy as well. Are you ready to be rescued?

We love because He first loved us (1 John 4:19).

Jennifer Mersberger is an Amazon Top 15 Christian author, public speaker, and founder of Lamplight Ministry. Through her Bible studies and weekly blog, Jennifer uses her unique perspective and fun sense of humor to help you see God in your everyday. Get to know her at *lamplightministry.com* and *Facebook.com/JenniferMersberger*.

Relocation

LeAnn Weiss-Rupard

Many are the plans in a person's heart, but it is the LORD's purpose that prevails (Proverbs 19:21).

Before I married Rick at age 42, I lived in Florida for 35 years. Rick works in the natural gas industry which has very few job opportunities in Florida. As an author, it was more practical for me to relocate. Even though I deeply loved my husband, I realized that the move from Orlando to beautiful rural New Mexico was going to be a difficult transition.

I'm a die-hard people person. Being around people energizes me. My new hometown of Aztec, New Mexico had a population a little larger than my church of nearly 5,000 back in Orlando. A grocery store, hardware store, a few mom & pop restaurants, and a small downtown of several blocks comprised my new neighborhood. It was a twenty minute round-trip drive just to pick up our mail and a four hour drive to the airport if the roads weren't blocked with ice or snow.

Unlike a stereotypical writer, I've never liked isolation or solitude. But, our premarital counselor, Dwight Bain, suggested that Rick's remote home would give us time to focus on each other without outside distractions. While Rick was at work 45 minutes away, my new life consisted of our dog Hoppy, and my 17, 23, & 25 year old stepsons on our secluded country acreage.

Rick and I talked about eventually transferring to Rick's home state of Texas. Meanwhile, Rick received a call from another company in Cleburne, Texas, for a position he hadn't even applied for.

Just before our first anniversary, we headed to Texas for the interview. After Rick received the job offer to move to Cleburne, we prayed about the possible move. As much as I wanted to escape the seclusion of New Mexico, I wanted to be where God wanted us to be. We both had doubts if it was the right time to relocate in the middle of a recession when the formerly booming housing market was sluggish.

That night I prayed, "Heavenly Father, you tell us to ask you when we lack wisdom. Please give us peace where you want us to live. If you want us to stay in New Mexico, we are willing. If you want Rick to work in Cleburne, please make it abundantly clear."

While I was praying, my computer chimed, "You've got mail." Minutes later, I opened my new email and saw that I had just received a Google News Alert on encouragement. The first article was titled "Reaching for the Sky" from the Cleburne Times.

"It couldn't be about Cleburne, Texas?" I wondered as I opened the article link. Cleburne, Texas, is a small town about 30 minutes southwest of Fort Worth, Texas. I had never heard of Cleburne before Rick's call. When I opened the story, the first thing I read was "Cleburne Times-Review, Cleburne, TX." After I told Rick about the email, we both experienced God's peace as we headed out to get moving boxes.

LeAnn Weiss-Rupard founded Encouragement Company in 1994 and has utilized her gift for lifting up and promoting others as a bestselling author, inspirational speaker, and political consultant. Her paraphrased Scriptures have been featured in over 10 million copies in addition to a greeting card line. She also wrote *Hugs for Friends* and the *Heartlifters* ™ series. Her last name changed July 4, 2008 when she married Rick Rupard. Contact her at *ECblessing@cs.com* or on Facebook at */leann.weissrupard*.

Loving an Unlovable World

Angie McCoy

F or God so loved the world that He gave His one and only Son, that whoever believes in Him shall not perish but have eternal life (John 3:16).

I'm sitting in a hotel room two days before Christmas and have pulled the Bible out of the drawer (Thank you, Gideons, for your faithful service). Before turning to Luke to read about the birth of the Prince of Peace, I'm intrigued by several pages of translated text in the pages preceding Genesis. It's John 3:16, translated into a few dozen languages.

We know this verse so well. It's the foundation of our faith in 25 words. But I read these words anew—*for God so loved the world*—and suddenly am faced with a hard truth and a challenge. God so loves the world, each and every six billion of us. He so loves the unlovable. He so loves the hateful, spiteful and hard-headed. He so loves those who mock Him, ignore Him, and deny Him.

For God so loved the world... Not just the peacemakers, the faithful, the broken-but-still-believing among us.

For God so loved the world... The words turn around in my head and heart and I wonder, "Do I love this world that God loves so much?" No, I do not.

I once had a friend who intentionally terminated relationships with people in her life when communication had become too strained. The relationships were so burdened by years of baggage, she said, she could no longer carry them. She didn't want her decision to go unnoticed, so she wrote letters to those handful of family members and friends she'd decided to let go.

Her approach seemed drastic to me at the time and, years later, still does. The truth is, though, at some point in our lives, most of us terminate relationships. We call less often and make excuses for not visiting. We let a river of disagreement grow into a canyon of division too broad to traverse. Or we allow a family member to terminate the relationship, deciding not to be the one to continue *working it out*.

Do we have good reason? Of course. They're uncompromising, wrong, implacable, _____ (fill in the blank).

But then, *God so loved the world...*

How can we accept the gift of the Prince of Peace, given to us at great cost to God out of His love for us, when we choose not to love those who've been placed in our lives? How can we find peace when division marks our family trees?

Several verses after John 3:16, John the Baptist is responding to those insisting that Jesus is somehow stealing his show. John responds in verse 30, "He must increase, but I must decrease." So it is with us. When we allow Jesus to fill us, our grievances decrease and we can begin to see others as God sees them: imperfect creatures ... just like us.

Angie McCoy is a freelance business writer serving clients in a variety of industries. Before creating her own business, she worked for large companies such as Kimberly-Clark, where she managed corporate communications, oversaw executive communications, and created and wrote online newsletters.

Peace for the Taking

Karen Ambler

She was my side kick. My shadow. My Partner-in-Crime. My confidant. My Best Friend. My Beloved One. To everyone else, she was just a rather scrawny little cat. To me, she was one of God's greatest gifts. Nine months after I made the monumental mistake of marrying an abusive man, she waltzed unannounced into my life bringing with her the comfort and true companionship which I so desperately needed. How like God to grant me such a grace-filled blessing after I committed such an epic failure.

He used this furry angel, aptly named Fuzzy, to get me through eight years of abuse and countless heartaches, and ultimately to accompany me on my escape from this cruel man. That first night of freedom, as I sat alone in my low-income housing feeling overcome with fear of the unknown, I clung to her warm, purring body for dear life.

And now, many far-happier years later, that 20 year old body was showing the signs of fraying at the edges. Old age and kidney disease were taking their toll. She had always been a slight bit of nothing, but tough as nails, and strong. Now weak and even skinnier, I became the comforter. If I could have purred for her, I gladly would have.

While doing everything possible to care for her and keep her free from pain, one emotion dominated my thoughts: Dread. I knew what was coming—she was going to die and there was no other way for this to end. Would I have to make a tough decision for mercy, or would the Lord take her breath while she slept? When and how would it happen? And most of all, how on earth would my heart bear the pain of such a loss?

Almost instinctively, I prayed for peace. Constantly. "Peace, Lord, please give me peace," I cried. I waited for it. Nothing. I pleaded some more, "Please, God, You said you would give peace and I need it now!" Still nothing but a heart filled with anxiety, as thoughts of doom shadowed my mind like ominous storm clouds.

Finally one quiet day, while I sat cradling my beloved pet, I was still long enough to hear the Lord speak clearly into my spirit. "Yes, I promised to give you peace, but you must *take* it." Take it? Well, I was asking for it, wasn't that enough? No. The God we serve is always a gentleman. Even what we ask for, He will not force upon us, but instead will hold it out freely for our taking. He helped me realize I was not accepting His gift of peace. I quickly changed my prayer from, "Give me peace," to "Help me, Jesus, to accept the peace you freely offer." *Peace I leave with you; my peace I give you. I do not give to you as the world gives. Do not let your hearts be troubled and do not be afraid* (John 14:27). The peace in this scripture is subjective. It is given by Jesus, but must be taken by the subject— His people—for it to be effective. I decided there and then to open my heart to His peace.

Shortly thereafter, the dreaded day came. My dear, precious baby peacefully fell asleep in Jesus even before the veterinarian had finished administering the merciful injections. Surely my heart broke with grief, but the strangest thing happened. I was overcome with peace. Peace not as the world gives, but the indescribable, unfathomable peace that comes from heaven alone. My heart was open to it, accepting of it, and God generously flooded it to overflowing. Just as He promised and right on time.

Karen Ambler's passion is helping women discover their true identity in Christ and find freedom through His Word. Karen mentors and leads Bible studies through her home-based ministry "For the Joy." She also ministers to hurting people with her registered therapy dog, Bendito, through Blessed Be Animal Assisted Therapy. Contact Karen at *blessedbeforthejoy.com*.

Pursue Peace

Lisa Burkhardt Worley

Every day something tries to disrupt our peace. It might be an argument at home, an unruly child or a work issue that snatches the peace from us. Then we spend the rest of the day fretting, rather than peaceful.

But didn't Jesus say, *Peace I leave with you, my peace I give you?* If He left it for us, why is it so hard to obtain?

This week I found the answer to that mysterious question in Colossians 3:15: *Let the peace of Christ rule in your hearts, since as members of one body you were called to peace.*

Let the peace of Christ RULE in your hearts. How could I have missed this? When we let life's troubles take over our minds, resulting in angst and worry, we are letting those troubles rule us, rather than peace.

Peace is not passive! We have to take action in order to have it and we have to choose to let it rule us, not our circumstances. Peace is not going to come on its own. Instead of saying, "Why don't I have peace?" we have to pursue it and consciously live above our scenarios that try to rob our peace. But how do we do that? I think Isaiah 26:3 provides some insight: *You will keep in perfect peace him whose mind is steadfast, because he trusts in You.*

Our minds must focus on the things of God, not of the world, and if our lives are centered on Him, we have to trust Him to work out our difficulties. Trust brings us peace, then peace rules, not worry.

The Hebrew word for trust also means "believe." Do

you believe God can handle your difficulties? Do you believe God wants the best for you? Do you trust God even when He has allowed you to be in the midst of a situation that, in your mind, does not make sense? That's a place God loves to take me and He asks, "When are you going to finally let go of your worldly wisdom and trust my wisdom, Lisa?"

If we trust and believe and live in the things from above, peace will come.

What about you, do you pursue peace or have you been waiting for it to come to you?

Lisa Burkhardt Worley is a Christian motivational speaker and writer and is the founder of Pearls of Promise Ministries, *pearlsofpromiseministries.com*. She is the co-author of the award winning manuscript, *If I Only Had...Following God's Path to Your Security*, and is an editor for the *Pearls of Promise* devotional. Follow her on Twitter *@pearlsofpromise*.

Pearls of Forgiveness

The Artist's Touch

By Lisa Buffaloe

A beautiful six inch cross sits on my dresser. My friend, Patricia, is a fused-glass artist. To create her crosses, she must carefully choose each glass based on what colors will appear after they have been subjected to the firing process. Seventy-five pieces are individually chosen, hand-cut, and perfectly shaped. No mold is used, and no two of her creations are exactly alike. The process and product is amazing—ordinary glass becomes a work of art.

If I took those same pieces, I could formulate an absolute mess. However from the hands of an artist, comes beauty.

Within each of us are pieces of good and bad memories, events, and influences. I didn't want to keep any of my "bad" pieces. I wanted to hide them away, throw them out, or pretend they didn't exist. Fortunately I can receive forgiveness for the bad things I have done, but what about all the pain and suffering caused by others?

Remember those glass pieces which are one color before the heat of the furnace? The fire brings out new hues, depth, and beauty. God is the artist. He takes our messed up lives, mends our wounds, and with His unfailing love, fires through the broken pieces and creates beauty.

God uses everything in amazing ways when we allow Him to walk us through and provide soul healing. And then if we are willing, He uses our difficulties to help in the battle for others. What better way to defeat the enemy, than turn the evil used against us to provide freedom for others?

All around us, people are dying—mentally, physically, and spiritually. And our stories may well be part of their rescue. No moment of your time, pain, or suffering is wasted. And you, as a work of art, are part of God's beautiful creation.

He has made everything beautiful in its time... (Ecclesiastes 3:11).

Lisa Buffaloe is writer, blogger, speaker, founder and host for Living Joyfully Free Radio. She is the author of *Nadia's Hope* (2010 Women of Faith Writing Contest Finalist), *Prodigal Nights* (2011 Women of Faith Writing Contest Finalist), *Grace for the Char-Baked,* and a contributing author of *The One Year Devotional of Joy and Laughter.*

Forgive and Forget?

By Beth Shriver

And when you stand praying, if you hold anything against anyone, forgive them, so that your Father in heaven may forgive you your sins (Mark 11:25).

On our way to church one Sunday we stopped at Starbucks. To my dismay, the woman in front of me in line was a person who mistreated my daughter. The saying *there are no coincidences with God* went through my mind as I stood within inches of this person. I told myself to let it go, forgive and forget, but it wasn't from the heart.

As our pastor gave a sermon on forgiveness, I sat in the pew thinking of the woman I'd just seen. It was a dark time for our family, so I'd stuffed it away in the back of my mind. So, I made myself look back on that time through God's eyes because the way I had dealt with it made me bitter. A quote from Nelson Mandela summed it up perfectly,

"Resentment is like drinking poison and then hoping it will kill your enemies."

But the really tough one was the pastor's definition of mercy. It was spot-on:

"Mercy is getting what you don't deserve."

I was defensive at first, thinking of this person getting away with what they did, and then it turned around on me. Who am I *not* to forgive when *I'm* a sinner? That little voice went off in my head, which is what I ask the Holy Spirit to do when asking for guidance. But I don't always want to listen.

Pastor talked about why it's so hard to forgive. These heart-breakers should be punished, not forgiven. But his response to that was to let God take care of the consequences. Mahatma Gandhi said, "The weak can't forgive."

But what about the emotional pain that we go through? What do we do with that constant reminder? It hurt tremendously when a chunk of windshield glass flew into my shoulder during a car accident. But the pain eventually went away, even though the scar is still there. We heal and hopefully move on. The scar is our badge of honor, for forgiving, even when someone didn't earn it. Because that someone is also me.

Faith Step: Make three columns:

- The name of the person to forgive
- What they did
- What you're going to do

Question: What do your three columns look like?

Beth Shriver is the author of *Annie's Truth, Grace Given* and *Healing Grace.* Her website is *BethShriverWriter.com.*

Confession Brings Healing

Lisa Burkhardt Worley

This week someone came back into my life to confess an offense that happened over thirty years ago. Truth be told, I carried that offense with me through all the years and it probably affected future relationships, so I was shocked to hear from him. However, I was pleased to know that he, too, had become a Christian during the course of the three decades. He had carried the guilt of his action against me for all this time; but it was only through the Lord's power that he was able to find me and say he was sorry.

God never intends us to carry a weighed down bag of guilt throughout our lives. That's why He tells us in Matthew 11:30: *For my yoke is easy and my burden is light.*

The Lord also exhorts us in James 5:16: *Therefore confess your sins to each other and pray for each other so that you may be healed. The prayer of a righteous man is powerful and effective.*

Confession is good for the soul and body. It can heal an open wound that has been seeping for years. It can make the burden light.

Is there any burden you have been carrying around for a long time and you cannot shake it from your mind? Does someone come to mind that you need to ask for forgiveness?

First, confess it to God and ask Him what to do

about it. You might also seek counsel from a couple of close Christian friends. It's possible the Lord may want you to face the person you offended.

No matter how long it has been, if the offense was great, I guarantee the offended person has not forgotten it. Making things right with a brother or sister may give closure to the situation.

May God richly bless your journey into confession and forgiveness.

Lisa Burkhardt Worley is a Christian motivational speaker and writer and is the founder of Pearls of Promise Ministries, *pearlsofpromiseministries.com*. She is the co-author of the award winning manuscript, *If I Only Had...Following God's Path to Your Security*, and is an editor for the *Pearls of Promise* devotional. Follow Lisa on Twitter *@pearlsofpromise*.

Intimacy Through Authenticity

Stacy Voss

I stepped on yet another toy in my daughter's Pepto-Bismol-pink bedroom this evening. "Ouch," I quickly yelped as Barbie drove her plastic foot into mine. "Micayla, how many times have I told you not to leave your toys on the floor?"

Before I could even finish my sentence, "I'm sorry. Can you please forgive me?" echoed throughout the room. Her intense, desperate look further demonstrated my daughter's great desire to receive my pardon. There was no way I could withhold it from her.

"Of course I forgive you, sunshine," I assured her, wrapping her in my arms.

I once believed that apologizing was a sign of weakness, acknowledging to self your shortcomings and then repeating them to another. I never would have imagined it would take my young daughter to show me the opposite is true. Apologizing requires courage because it offers the other a chance to accept or reject your most personal invitation. Yet it is also the most incredible gift one can give to another, an opportunity into deeper, more authentic relationship.

As I see my daughter continually repeat this scenario, I'm beginning to understand that admitting my mistakes and asking for forgiveness doesn't make me a bad person. To the contrary, it paves the way for a deeper, more trusting relationship with others.

Admitting my wrongdoings has also freed me to be more intimate in my relationship with Christ. No longer do I have to come pretending to have it all together, something that is such a far cry from reality that I could no longer keep up the facade. Instead, I get to come as I am, a mess and all, apologize for what I've done, and know I'll receive Christ's forgiveness even faster than I could offer it to my sweet girl. There is nothing more beautiful than that!

But if we confess our sins to Him, He is faithful and just to forgive us our sins and to cleanse us from all wickedness (1 John 1:9).

May we freely extend and receive forgiveness.

Stacy Voss is the founder of Eyes of Your Heart Ministries (*eyesofyourheart. com*). She is known for her ability to bring biblical characters and principles to life in thought-provoking, transformative ways. She lives in Colorado with her husband and their two energetic kids.

Once Bitten

Jennifer Mersberger

I had my first run-in with fire ants when I was a little girl. My best friend, Julie, and I decided to explore in the field at the end of the block. As we walked across the parched ground, my foot gave way into softer soil. Within seconds my foot was covered with hostile fire ants. Together, we managed to wipe the ants off, but only after we endured countless bites.

My foot felt numb as we hurried home. My mom knew how to help me feel better. But by the end of the day, sores had formed all around my toes. We were told not to remove the poison from the bites so I endured the pain. Those bites left scars on my foot for years.

We can get emotionally bitten as well. The sting of harsh words can send venom coursing through our spirit. The more bites we receive, the greater the impact. And as long as the poison stays within us, it causes damage.

Now that I'm older, I know if I don't remove the venom from an ant bite it will scar my skin. But how do we remove the venom from being bitten by others? We forgive them. But first we need to give a little TLC to our spirit when we're attacked emotionally. Words hurt.

Cry if you need to. I wailed like a baby as those ants attacked me. It hurt and I cried out in pain. So allow yourself a few cleansing tears. But then evaluate what was said: Is it true? Does what they're saying align with God's word? Would God Himself say that about you? Were you in the wrong? Is it possible that their comment really has more to do with them and less to do with you? In other words, were you caught in the crossfire of their own emotional battle? What else could have motivated them to say what they said?

Then finally, forgive them for it. We are all human, flawed and imperfect. We all make mistakes and say things we wish we could take back. I know I have! It breaks my heart to think my careless words could cause an emotional scar. But they can. For all the times I've been bitten, there are several times when I've been the ant. *Lord, please forgive my foolish words.*

Are you nursing the wound of a pretty bad bite? Are you ready to get rid of the poison inside? Pray God's word and allow Him to speak truth into your life. It is healing ointment for the soul...

All kinds of animals, birds, reptiles and creatures of the sea are being tamed and have been tamed by man, but no man can tame the tongue. It is a restless evil, full of deadly poison.

With the tongue we praise our Lord and Father, and with it we curse human beings, who have been made in God's likeness (James 3:9).

Jennifer Mersberger is an Amazon Top 15 Christian author, public speaker, and founder of Lamplight Ministry. Through her Bible studies and weekly blog, Jennifer uses her unique perspective and fun sense of humor to help you see God in your everyday. Get to know her at *lamplightministry.com* and *Facebook.com/JenniferMersberger.*

Letting Go

Patty Mason

I've had many regrets in life, and perhaps the biggest one is how I saw life during a season of depression. I made choices, spoke words, did things, and acted in ways that placed a mark of shame on my soul. Forgiving someone who has harmed you is hard. But, all too often, it's even harder to forgive yourself.

In order to find freedom, I had to admit my mistakes and forgive myself for all of the hurt and pain I imposed on others.

I had to first forgive myself for all the choices I made, like drinking while my children were around, or leaving them unattended while I went to sleep off another dark day of depression. I had to forgive myself for the desire to take my own life, and leave my family behind to deal with the loss and aftermath. I had to forgive myself so I could move forward, and allow my family and God to forgive me.

My first step toward forgiveness and healing was to admit the hurt I caused. It was hard to confront the way I unleashed my repressed anger upon my oldest child. It broke my heart to think about how I lashed out at her. But if I was to forgive myself and receive forgiveness from others, I had to acknowledge the pain. My daughter was very young at the time; I recall the day I shared my heartfelt remorse with her. Immediately, this little girl began to cry. She threw her arms around my waist, looked up at me and said, "I didn't think you loved me."

It's been almost 16 years since that time, and I am

grateful for the relationship I now share with my daughter. Peace and joy flood my soul with healing, and my past regrets no longer weigh me down with despair.

We all have times when we make mistakes. Times when we've said things or done things we wish we hadn't—things we would take back in a minute if we could. Maybe you feel responsible for the place where you now find yourself. Perhaps the things you've tried to keep quiet have haunted your soul. There are many choices we make, some may even cause us to feel shame or even self-hatred. I know it's hard, but if you are the one you need to forgive, allow me to encourage you to take a step toward healing through forgiveness. Your mistakes do not have to hold you back one more day. Admit you were wrong. Take responsibility for the pain and ask for forgiveness. First ask God to forgive you and to help you. Then ask those you hurt to forgive you, and then let all the pain go and forgive yourself.

Patty Mason is an author who has written three books: *Transformed by Desire: A Journey of Awakening to Life and Love; Finally Free: Breaking the Bonds of Depression without Drugs; Experiencing Joy: Strategies for Living a Joy Filled Life.* Patty's website is *libertyinchristministries.com.*

One and Two-Sided Forgiveness

Anne Shannon

The other day I was chatting with a friend and told her about forgiving someone who had hurt me as a child. She seemed amazed that I could forgive this person, and I looked at her and asked, "How could I not forgive, as I have been forgiven so much?"

Forgiveness is something I've had quite a bit of experience with, and I know that the freedom found in forgiving is worth the effort it takes to put the matter aside.

Forgiveness is not always two-sided. Most of my experience with forgiveness has been choosing to forgive someone who hasn't asked for it. As long as I allow hurt feelings, a betrayal, or a social slight to preoccupy me, I cannot focus on God's greatest commandment.

Teacher, which is the greatest commandment in the Law? Jesus replied, "Love the Lord your God with all your heart and with all your soul and with all your mind. This is the first and greatest commandment. And the second is like it: Love your neighbor as yourself. All the Law and the Prophets hang on these two commandments" (Matthew 22:36-40).

By forgiving and releasing a situation, I am able to love God and my neighbor with all of my heart, soul and mind.

Recently, I experienced forgiveness that was two-sided. A very dear friend and I experienced a break in our relationship. We were both going through a rough patch, and she chose to let the relationship go. Because we attended the same church, we still saw each other on a regular basis. During this time, God taught me that if I fully relied on Him, He would repair our relationship. At one point I thought to myself, "If she would just apologize, everything would be fine." The problem with that line of thinking is that mine are the only thoughts I can control, so I began to pray, "Lord, if it is your will that she apologize, please lay it upon her heart to do so, but if this is not your will, please release my need for it."

After praying this for several months, God released my need for the apology and our friendship began to heal. One day, while having coffee, she surprised me by saying, "God has placed you on my heart a lot recently. I want you to know that I treated you very badly. You didn't deserve it and I hope you will forgive me." In an instant the last fragments of the wound in my heart smoothed over and our friendship was fully restored. Some will say a friendship can never be the same after a break like the one we experienced; I would say they are right, but not the way they intended. Instead, it is even more precious than before.

After 12 years in the corporate world, **Anne Shannon** was called home to homeschool and care for her two teenage daughters. Anne is passionate about raising Godly children in a world, which is sometimes ungodly. Anne's life goal is to encourage others through acts of compassion and kindness.

Regrets Only

Cathy Biggerstaff

"**R**egrets Only" the invitation read in the space where RSVP normally resided. Trying to meld this phrase which conjures up negative emotions and the festivity of a party or wedding left me puzzled. So few people respond to an RSVP these days, I can't imagine anyone would call saying, "No, we're not coming." The interaction would force an excuse. I had a pastor who said he had quit telling people he missed seeing them in church on Sunday because it seemed to obligate a response and he didn't want to be the cause of folks having to lie to him.

"Regrets Only" can apply to relationships. A former dear friend died recently and I felt deep regret at her passing. She was still a young woman at age fifty-five and I regretted her seven-month battle with cancer. A few months before her diagnosis, she had retired and was excited to see where God would lead her next. Her treatments started the day she was diagnosed. My main regret was that our friendship had waned a few months before she was diagnosed.

We became fast friends when we attended Lay Speaker Training together. Over the next four years, we were in two intense thirty-six week Bible studies and my husband and I attended the Couples Bible Study she and her husband hosted. We led worship together at a local nursing home once a month and were both part of a year-long leadership development program for small membership Methodist churches.

And then the unthinkable happened. An innocent incident at church escalated into pure ugliness.

Devastation caused my family to leave the church we had loved and supported and been an active part of for thirty-three years. We could not sit in the pew and worship with people who thought taking the Biblical approach to reconciliation was NOT the right thing to do.

Although my friend and I made an attempt to save our relationship, it was never the same again. I forgave her, we had lunch together, were surface friendly but we'd lost the depth in our relationship.

The Greek word for regret is *metamelomai* and occurs six times in the New Testament. It means to experience a change of concern after a change of emotion, usually causing us to fall into emotional remorse afterwards. Repentance is tied to regret, causing us to understand that the thing we regret included some sort of sin.

Per Isaiah 9:6, Jesus was born to bring order to my life, to be my Wonderful Counselor, my Mighty God, my Everlasting Father and my Prince of Peace through all of life's ups and downs. Do you have regrets in your life? I suppose we all do. How did you work through yours? Think back: was there sin involved in the situation you regret? Did you repent and find freedom? My Wonderful Counselor and Prince of Peace helped me through mine and He will bring you through yours.

Cathy Biggerstaff, a Christian clown, blogs weekly at *cathybiggerstaff. blogspot.com* and would love for you to visit and follow her Joyful Journey. She writes children's books, curriculum, and devotionals. Cathy is published in *Mature Living Magazine,* on *ChristianDevotions.us,* and she guest blogs.

The Thanksgiving Miracle

Sandra Marchel

It was with great expectation and excitement that we prepared our home for our family gathering at Thanksgiving. As each family member arrived at our home, the anticipation heightened as to what I believed would occur at this gathering. Since it had been years since we had been together as a family, I envisioned long-held desires for family unity would become a reality. It was only after I reflected on the time we'd spent together that I realized my expectations were unrealistic. I remember experiencing feelings of defeat as I re-counted the events and conflict that occurred that day, yet in my heart wondered if we had truly experienced a breakthrough.

The people were encouraged in Joshua 3:5 to *sanctify themselves, for tomorrow the Lord will do wonders among you* (KJV). To sanctify is to set ourselves apart from that which would hinder us from living our lives as Christ lived His. In light of the events of the weekend, I sensed I was to seek the Lord and lead my family in pursuit of resolution and restoration. God's Word encouraged me to focus on Him and His approach to conflict by allowing His influence alone to impact my decisions. By His grace, I was enabled to submit my emotions, reasoning and feelings of disappointment, hurt, seeming failure, offense and unforgiveness to Him. By His strength, I was fortified to stand strong and not be moved by the opinions or fears of others. By His Spirit, I was empowered to resist the temptation to deny, ignore or give in to the problem. And through His encouragement and wisdom, I was able to resist the lies of the enemy, finding confidence to embrace the hope that God would use these events to bring about good in all of our lives.

Since that weekend, I'm encouraged by the openness in each of our hearts to pursue reconciliation. Each day of connecting with one another tears down walls that have been in existence for years. Little by little, our hearts have become more open to one another. Breakthrough, defined as "a significant and dramatic overcoming of a perceived obstacle, which allows the completion of a process," did occur that weekend in the birthing of a new beginning for our family. We have, as a family, confronted the enemy of division by pursuing the resolution of conflict. Though a significant and dramatic obstacle was presented, we as a family are overcoming it by God's grace. In endeavoring to resolve our differences by recognizing that our individual strengths and weaknesses make us strong as we yield to one another, we become more unified. Unrealistic expectations have been transformed into realistic dreams and desires as we embrace one another with genuine love, acceptance and forgiveness. The strength of the obstacle that came against us is the strength in family unity that is being realized as our hearts are being knit together with His love.

Sandra Marchel is a free-lance writer who has had devotions published in *The Upper Room Daily Devotional Guide.*

Free to Forgive

Wendy Saxton

They dress the wound of my people as though it were not serious. 'Peace, peace,' they say, when there is no peace (Jeremiah 6:14).

For years, I tried and failed to forgive the men who'd harmed me. Pro-active by nature, I read books, received counseling, and highlighted all the pertinent verses in my Bible. Yet despite my sincerity, I remained captive to toxic emotions—which often gave way to destructive behavior. So I'd double my efforts (surely one day my emotions will yield to the forgiveness I've proclaimed), then watch the months fly off the calendar.

It's the nature of God to comfort His children when we're hurting. My comfort came in the form of a scripture that didn't command forgiveness, but rather, validated my pain. According to Jeremiah 6:14, God took my wounds seriously. Had I?

This passage inspired me to set aside time each day to sit in a quiet place with Jesus and confess the contents of my heart. The pain. The rage. The confusion. I stopped saying, "Peace, peace" when I had no peace. I told Him where I hurt, why I hurt—and how I'd hurt others as a result of the pain. As I confessed, He gathered the fragments of my heart. As He gathered, He healed. And the more He healed, the more compelled I was to pray, *Jesus, will you forgive me for attempting to guard and heal my wounds in my own strength?*

Not long after that prayer, He prompted me to forgive the men who'd abused me. And for the first time in my life I had it to give. It was like finding money in my pocket. Hey, how'd that get there! It was there because He put it there. Christ transformed my heart into a place from which forgiveness flows, just as He commands in Matthew 18:35. The Great Physician knew earlier my heart was too broken to forgive.

He never minimizes the circumstances that break our hearts. We do, when we deny Him access to the pain.

Father in heaven, thank You for taking my wounds seriously. What happened to me does not go unseen in your eyes. Provide shelter under your wing when I come to you hurting and confused. Grant me the resolve to return to you with my whole heart, and deliver me from the pressure of believing that it must happen all at once. Uphold my baby steps with grace, and cover my mistakes with mercy. The world is a dangerous place for a girl. Reveal the refuge in being your daughter, and lead me into the path of righteousness, where healing and forgiveness flow freely. In Jesus' name, amen.

Wendy Saxton is a writer and speaker. She shares her story about forgiveness at *wendysaxton.com*.

Pearls of Trust

Cracks in the Sidewalk

Lisa Burkhardt Worley

Recently I took a walk by myself and spent a lot of time admiring nature and listening to God. At one point, I asked the Lord to give me a new devotion idea for my blog.

All I heard was "Cracks in the sidewalk."

"Cracks in the sidewalk?" What does that mean? There was no answer initially, but I began to study the cracks in the sidewalk as I walked, and I realized there was a message there.

Even though the sidewalk was taking me to my ultimate destination, there were still cracks along the way. I knew it was the right sidewalk, so I had to remain on it despite the cracks. I remember one time when I tried to take a shortcut around a sidewalk, I fell in a hole, covered up by grass, and sprained my ankle.

Don't we do that in our lives? We want to avoid the cracks? When we do, sometimes we fall into a pit!

If you're a writer like me, the crack in the sidewalk may be a delay in publishing the book you've been called to write, or an illness or injury that sets you back. If you've surrendered your life to Christ and are certain of your calling, a crack doesn't mean you need to change sidewalks for a smoother journey. God calls us to remain on the path He has set out for us.

Psalm 37:23-24 says: *The LORD makes firm the steps*

of the one who delights in Him; though he may stumble, he will not fall, for the LORD *upholds him with His hand.*

Yes, we may stumble over the cracks in our sidewalks, but God's desire for us is to persevere and trust Him even when the path becomes uneven.

Lisa Burkhardt Worley is a former national television sports reporter who is now a founder/writer/speaker with Pearls of Promise Ministries, *pearlsofpromiseministries.com.* She is the co-author of the award winning manuscript, *If I Only Had...Following God's Path to Your Security* and co-editor of the *Pearls of Promise* devotional. Pearls of Promise is on Facebook at */pearlsofpromiseministries.*

G's House

Catherine Weiskopf

Our house on Bershire fit us like a pair of tight jeans after an all you can eat buffet. We needed breathing room, but with our mess, if we wanted a bigger house we would have to buy a new house before selling the old. It made my husband and I both nervous, but we tentatively stepped out into the housing market.

A month later, we put in a low offer on a tree laden house that was just right and they surprised us by taking it. We would soon be the proud owners of two houses, two electric bills, and two nervous hearts! What were we thinking? We were the couple who ordered water at restaurants and wore holey underwear to save money.

At this point, I knew, intellectually, that if God wanted us to move it would be ok, but trusting His provision felt like diving off a cliff into unknown waters.

The day of packing, a neighbor came over to chat and share good news. "We sold our house to a couple paying cash," Farrine said. They had thought they found the perfect house, but air conditioner trouble had caused them to back out.

"I'm not sure where we're going to live," Farrine said, explaining that they couldn't find another house in time.

Without thinking the words tumbled out of my mouth. "You can live in our house. It'll be empty soon," I said.

And so, a few weeks later, as our boxes of toddler

toys moved out, their boxes of girl paraphernalia moved in. In the meantime I still worried about the money siphon of owning two houses.

About a month later the Pico's found another house and once again boxes were starting to be packed at our house on Bershire. It was then another friend stopped by our new house to get moving boxes.

Their house had been on the market for "too long," but had finally sold. Coral had found a house her family really liked, but it was being built. "The house won't be ready in time," Coral explained.

Again the words tumbled out, "You can live in our house until your house is ready," I said. "The Pico's are moving out."

And so as the Pico's boxes moved out and the Toleman's boxes moved in. It was then that all my worries about financial loss evaporated. Clearly God was using our house and when He was done, it would sell.

A month later, when the Toleman's got ready to move out, I wondered what God would do next? The phone rang and it was our realtor. "We have an offer on the house and for more money than you have it on the market for," he said.

I laughed as I realized God was speaking directly to all my worries and anxieties saying, "Trust Me."

Our neighbors called our one story house on Bershire the Gypsy house, but I prefer another name: "God's House."

Catherine Weiskopf is creative director of Pearls of Promise Ministries. She is the author of math books for elementary students, *Lemon & Ice & Everything Nice* from Scholastic and co-author of the cartoon illustrated *Adventures in Mathopolis* series. Check out her books at *cweiskopf.com.*

Light My Path

Janna Longfellow Hughes

T hy word is a lamp unto my feet and a light unto my path (Psalm 119:105 KJV).

The blackness of the night sky obliterated everything as I struggled to open the front door of my house. When it gave way to my persistence, I stumbled over something. "Ouch! My toe." I would have jumped around but didn't want to crash into anything else.

Once inside, I turned on the light. Everything became clear.

These circumstances reminded me of events in my personal finances. Previously, I had overspent and dropped myself into a dark hole. When the situation grew serious, friends suggested I study scriptures on handling money. I joined a group of others who were doing the same.

Over the course of weeks, ten of us prayed and studied thousands of verses related to finances. During these prayerful studies, the word of God challenged my thinking. My ideas and practices changed. Along with them my financial situation took a better course.

God's Word had literally become a lamp unto my feet and a light unto my path. When the light came on, it came from within. I could see the subtle hidden darkness of some of my previous practices.

God's powerful light enabled me to correct my course and quickly align my ways with His desires and instructions. I was no longer hobbling around in the darkness and stubbing my toe with debt and unnecessary expenditures. The light from His words in my heart guided me away from unsound actions and toward a better day.

Father help us to run to you for your light. Fill us with light. Help us to change our ways to do what pleases you. Amen.

Janna Longfellow Hughes is a television producer and published writer who can be found at *JannaLongfellowHughes.com*. Janna has also written an ebook, *DEVELOP YOUR STORY - Tools for Building a Bridge to Your Audience* (download free at Janna's website).

Fruit That Will Last

Rita Spruce

Earlier this year, I heard a speaker at a women's conference say something very shocking. She said, "God is trusting the planet to people like me." In that moment I knew that the Lord was confirming His will for my life. A seed He had already planted in my heart was being watered.

John 15:16 tells us, *You did not choose me, but I chose you and appointed you to go and bear fruit—fruit that will last.* We bring glory to God when we bear good fruit, but the thought of producing fruit pleasing to God is a daunting one. How could I produce anything good in myself that would be pleasing to God? A picture of a heavy-laden apple tree formed in my mind when I began to think about natural, fruit-bearing trees. Bearing good fruit isn't hard for an apple tree; it simply reproduces itself.

Jesus said, *I am the vine; you are the branches. If a man remains in me and I in him, he will bear much fruit; apart from me you can do nothing* (John 15:5).

Producing good fruit that lasts is a part of our spiritual DNA when we abide in Christ. The Creator created us to reproduce. We are not reproducing ourselves; we are reproducing Jesus who lives within us. When we are attached to the life-giving vine, our faith increases and our love grows. Deep roots are produced by endurance, which is inspired by hope in Christ alone.

At the beginning of this year, the Lord began whispering to me about a new field He wanted me to cultivate: a partnership with my husband in the fight against human trafficking. Proverbs 31:16 says, *She considers a field and buys it; out of her earnings she plants a vineyard.* For months I struggled, surveying the vast, hard ground of human trafficking, repeatedly asking a single question, "How can I help?" It was easy for my husband. After a long career devoted to justice on state, national, and international levels, my godly husband's passion for righteousness still produces fruit and his life's work against injustice continues in his long-tended field.

Through prayer, reading the Word, and listening for His still, small voice, I have come to know that my gifts perfectly compliment my husband's gifts. God is not asking me to bear the same kind of fruit as my husband; I am to bear my own fruit. My desire is to see people healed of their brokenness and restored to wholeness in Christ. I want others to live in the same kind of freedom that I enjoy. In partnering with my husband, the justice of God and the mercy of God meet in a shared field and we work together for a common harvest.

The life that God chooses for us isn't always easy; it requires radical obedience and courage. But know this: there are living, breathing people on the other side of our obedience and obedience bears fruit—fruit that will last.

Rita Spruce is co-founder of Disrupt Human Trafficking. Her website is *disruptht.org* and she can be found on Twitter *@disruptht*. ©2012 Rita Spruce.

In Whom Do You Trust?

Lisa Mick

In whom do you trust? Is it in yourself, someone else, or in God? Earlier in life, I trusted my earthly father. I adored him and wanted to do so much for him. I loved making chocolate chip cookies as they were his favorite treat.

My father was a deacon of our church and we were at the church every time the doors opened. However, as I grew up, some things changed in our house and home life became scary to me. As I look back, I realize when trust in my earthly father waned, trust in my heavenly Father grew.

One day when I came home from school, my father was wearing army fatigues, boots and a holster around his waist. The holster had a real pistol in it. Fear immediately set in and I wondered why he needed to carry around a pistol at all times? For his protection? For the family's protection?

My gun toting father made me believe someone was going to come in our house and hurt our family, so one night as I stood in my bedroom doorway, I started thinking about my safety. Staring out at the shag carpet with the dim moonlight shining down, it reminded me of water. My mind envisioned large crocodiles in the water that would protect me. So I started my usual run to my place of slumber. I was trying to not let the crocodiles touch me as I jumped into bed.

Even though I imagined the crocodiles, I was still scared. So was I putting my trust in the wrong thing? The crocodiles weren't eliminating my fear. Trusting my earthly dad also failed. So as a young girl I realized I needed to start turning my fears over to the Lord because nothing else worked. Since doing that, my heavenly Father has never left my side. I know He is my Protector, one in whom I trust. I have learned that He is my strength and my defense. As long as I trust HIM, my fear always subsides.

Surely God is my salvation; I will TRUST and not be afraid. The Lord, the Lord, is my strength and my defense: He has become my salvation. With joy you will draw water from the wells of salvation (Isaiah 12: 2-3).

Lisa Mick is director of outreach for Pearls of Promise Ministries and is also one of the editors for the *Pearls of Promise* devotional. Lisa is co-authoring a Bible study that helps non-writers to record their faith journey. She is a regular contributor to the Pearls of Promise blog and can be found on Facebook at */lisa.s.mick.3.*

Narrowing Your Focus

Mary Jane Downs

I was privileged to sit by an energetic mother of two on a flight to New Hampshire. As we talked, I found out Judy was already a Christian but she was frustrated with people calling her "narrow-minded" because of her faith in the Word of God. As I continued to listen to this young mother's search to be an example to her small boys, I began to pray for wisdom. Being a seasoned mother and believer myself, I wanted to help her receive something that would give her some peace of mind. Soon, the Lord's inspiration began to flow.

I started by telling Judy when people called her narrow-minded, she could actually consider that a compliment. She looked at me funny. Then she asked how.

I explained to Judy that she was narrowing her scope to focus only on Jesus and His words. She was funneling in what would help her grow and it was changing her perspectives. What others were seeing was a more purified version of her, one that glorified Christ and not her own selfish desires. In a roundabout way, others were actually validating her growth and giving her an opportunity to affirm her new lifestyle. Judy's countenance began to lift with a smile.

Next, I asked Judy if Christ-likeness was what she wanted to achieve? She said yes. Then I asked Judy if she wanted to proclaim the Christ living inside of her? She said yes. Last, I asked Judy if she wanted to go forward or turn back? She thought for a moment and then responded with forward. Then I stated again, if she would choose to think of narrow-mindedness in a more positive way, she could turn the situation around.

Finally, I challenged Judy to respond differently when called narrow-minded. Instead of getting upset, just smile and thank them for acknowledging the godly choices. This way of response instead of frustration might lead to a greater opportunity to witness the love of Christ. Your positive attitude, without judgment, could change the atmosphere and bring forth seeds of salvation planted in the lives of others.

Judy was meeting her goal of becoming more Christ-like by narrowing her focus to Jesus alone. She was bravely standing up for what she believed when others wanted to pull her down. The fact that others were taking notice could be made into a plus, if she would choose to look at those situations in a new way.

I keep my eyes always on the LORD. With Him at my right hand, I will not be shaken (Psalm 16:8).

Have you ever been called narrow-minded and formed a negative attitude about yourself and others? Looking at these situations in a more positive way could bring about a new freedom in your walk with Christ. The process begins as you make a quality decision first. Who do you desire to please more...Christ or the world?

Mary Jane Downs is an author, speaker and teacher who lives in the foothills of the Asheville Mountains. Her website is *maryjanewrites.com.*

Do You Really Listen To That Still Small Voice?

Lisa Mick

How many times have you heard the Holy Spirit, but questioned Him? Did you feel like you knew a better way? We have all been skeptical at times, but God finally convinced me to listen.

I was in a church meeting where positions of service were being discussed. I could do many of them, but there was a nagging feeling I was not going to be available when the time came to perform the task. I wanted to raise my hand to help, but the feeling would not subside. So what do you think I did?

I quieted the Holy Spirit and volunteered!

Have you ever done that my friend? When you hear that still small voice, do you really listen or do you tend to push forward in your own stubborn will? I tuned God out because I was worried about what others would think of me for not signing up.

Through this experience, God opened my eyes to my Counselor. I had to cancel all the jobs I signed up for. You see, that year my family needed me from one drama to the next. My brother had major back surgery and wanted me to be with him at the hospital. My son had an appendectomy, so I needed to spend time with him at the same hospital and time with him at home while he healed. Then, would you believe my other son broke his arm and he needed my help?

Now, if that wasn't enough, my mom had knee replacement surgery and I had to travel about 45 minutes one-way to see her in a rehabilitation center for several weeks and then move her into my home for about a month. This was all in a few months time period before and during Thanksgiving and Christmas.

Our sweet precious Lord helped me to understand when I hear that still small voice, my Counselor, I should stop, listen attentively and pray. There were three lessons I learned that day. One was I always need to listen to the Holy Spirit, my Counselor. The second was I need to be secure in my own world. I now realize no one was paying attention to what I was signing up for. After all, it's not all about me and if they questioned my not signing up, I have discerned that it would be their issue. The third most important nugget I gleaned was to pause, and pray about what God wanted me to do and sign up later only if I get the go-ahead from Him.

You can believe that now when I hear the small whisper inside my spirit, I listen. My friends, do you?

And I will ask the Father, and He will give you another advocate to help you and be with you forever—the Spirit of truth. The world cannot accept Him, because it neither sees Him nor knows Him. But you know Him, for He lives with you and will be in you (John 14:16-17).

Lisa Mick is director of outreach for Pearls of Promise Ministries and is also one of the editors for the *Pearls of Promise* devotional. Lisa is also co-authoring a Bible study helping non-writers to record their faith journey. She is a regular contributor to the Pearls of Promise blog and can be found on Twitter *@LisaGMick*.

God Knows His Plan

Carole Towriss

You are my hiding place; you will protect me from trouble and surround me with songs of deliverance (Psalm 32:7).

Submitting to God's plan for our life can be painful, even agonizing. I know. When we got married, my husband and I both wanted a large family. We started trying to get pregnant after we'd been married almost two years. Two years after that we saw a doctor, and spent six more years swallowing pills and getting shots. I prayed and cried, and cried and prayed. I hated Mother's Day. I was terrified of spending the rest of my life without a child. I'd see pregnant teenagers clearly not ready for motherhood, and abandoned babies, and abused children, and wonder why our prayers remained unanswered.

A few months ago a faithful Haitian man in our church died after a long battle with cancer. He'd dedicated his life to evangelizing the Haitian people in Washington, DC. He pastored the Creole-speaking church his father started, distributed Bibles, even resigned a lucrative job to drive a taxi to more actively share the Gospel. Last month his widow was diagnosed with breast cancer.

Stories like these don't seem fair.

Sometimes, in time, we can see a reason for God's actions.

We eventually had one bio child, and adopted three

more babies from Kazakhstan. We have a crazy, wacky set of four kids that share no DNA and very few traits, but make for a chaotic, fun, and love-filled house. Had we not brought them to our home, they most likely would never have heard the name of Jesus. Perhaps one day one of them will take it back there, and be able to share it as only native-born people can. Maybe not. Only God knows.

Sometimes we never see His plan.

My mother-in-law died shortly after we were married. I adored her. She was forever buying Bibles and giving them away. A couple of weeks after the funeral we received a call from the Christian bookstore saying a special order she had placed had arrived—Bibles. My children will never know her. I still can't see any reason for her death. Why would God take her? I still don't know. Only God knows.

Yes, submitting to the sovereignty of God's will can be bitter. But without trust in our heavenly Father, without believing He knows what He is doing, life will knock you down, take you out, and eventually destroy you. You can let life do that, or you can cling to the Rock. Even when you just can't understand, when you feel overwhelmed, God will hold you close. Say to Him, "Be my hiding place, my Refuge." He will. In the midst of all the uncertainty and anguish, I promise He will.

Carole Towriss is the author of *In the Shadow of Sinai,* a Biblical fiction released November 1, 2012 by DeWard Publishing Company. You can visit her at *caroletowriss.com.*

What's Your Nineveh?

Catherine Weiskopf

The word of the LORD came to Jonah son of Amittai: "Go to the great city of Nineveh and preach against it, because its wickedness has come up before me." But Jonah ran away from the LORD and headed for Tarshish (Jonah 1:1-3).

God spoke to Jonah and told him to get on his feet, out the door, and go and preach to the city of Nineveh. Jonah got to his feet, walked out the door and sprinted the other way. After all who wants to tell bad people to repent and end up as a sword shish kebab. It took an angry ocean and three nights in the belly of a whale to change his mind and obey.

Where do you not want to go with God? What's your Nineveh? Yours probably doesn't involve a sword but most likely it does involve some fear. God is asking you to do something—you're pretty sure about it. Something has been tugging at your heart for awhile. You may not run away physically, but you run away and try to quiet God's voice with busyness.

I know how Jonah felt because I ran away as well. I ran from flying on trips I felt called to make. I hated to fly as much as Jonah hated the trip to Nineveh. To most people a trip overseas does not feel like a life or death event but to me it did. Instead of pointy words and rock, my claustrophobic thoughts of hundreds of people stuck on a plane click in. So when my husband asked me to go to China with him, I made an excuse and got busy avoiding the conversation. Flying was my Nineveh.

I have a friend who has a beautiful voice. She sang and inspired people at church for years. Then one day when she was singing, her voice quaked and her hands began to shake. She had a panic attack right on stage. Now she's in the belly of the whale: she spends her time avoiding singing. Even her new friends have never heard her voice. If they did, they might ask her to sing in public. Singing in public is her Nineveh.

If you are currently in the body of the whale, struggling with fear, God wants you to know you are not alone. Fear has temporarily stopped many people including some of the holiest and best:

Elijah ran away to the cave (1 King 19: 1-18).

Moses argued about his assignment (Exodus 3:10-13).

Peter denied Christ (John 18:15-27).

The rest of their stories are:

Elijah came out of the cave and returned to do God's work.

Moses lost the argument and led the Israelites out of Egypt.

Peter became the rock on which Christ built His church.

They all learned that running, denying, and arguing only stopped them from living the glorious life God had planned for them.

Dear God, Help me to be obedient even when I am fearful.

Catherine Weiskopf is creative director of Pearls of Promise Ministries and is one of the editors for the *Pearls of Promise* devotional. She is a regular contributor to the Pearls of Promise blog and can be found on Twitter *@Cweiskopf.*

Dreams and Detours

Barbara Ferguson

I was living my dream at eighteen. Winning a national 4-H scholarship had made college possible. My single mother supported five children, so if I wanted to go to college, financing it was my responsibility. By working ten hours a week at the campus day care, I paid all expenses. In the spring, the counselors helped me obtain a tuition scholarship for my sophomore year. I was a new Christian; tuition was taken care of for the next year, and I'd be a home economics teacher in three years. Life was perfect and I looked forward to my sophomore year!

That summer I worked in the hospital kitchen making some extra cash for the upcoming year. After a couple of months lifting heavy pots in the hospital kitchen, the doctor immobilized my damaged right wrist with a splint. I was no longer a valuable employee, so I was terminated. This minimized the projected savings for college, and I couldn't care for all my needs away from home with one hand. With shattered dreams I moved home. *In his heart a man plans his course, but the Lord determines his steps* (Proverbs 16:9).

Fortunately my family lived in a college town, so I was able to continue my education. The University of New Mexico was within walking distance from our house and the scholarship transferred, so I enrolled full-time in the fall.

In mid-September I began to get sick every Sunday morning. If I didn't leave the choir and find a place to lie down soon enough, I passed out. Since our family had no car, I rode to church with a neighbor. After a couple of days in bed I would be able to return to class. By just dropping one course, I completed the semester. Had I been away at school, I would have had to return home, lost the credits for the semester, and forfeited the scholarship. I was beginning to learn that I can make plans, but only God knows the future.

As a young Christian, I joined a group of students who went to Boys Ranch every Friday night. We took refreshments and spent the evening playing games with the boys and sharing a Bible story. In the spring, several of the boys accepted Christ, and invited us to their church one Sunday night to witness their baptisms. On the way home, Len asked me for our first date. Sixteen months later we were married.

I'm glad God knew the wonderful future He had planned for me, when all I could see were painful circumstances I thought were roadblocks to my future. God taught me early on my spiritual journey that dreams are good, and we can trust God's GPS to guide us.

Trust in the Lord with all your heart and lean not to your own understanding. In all your ways submit to Him, and He will make your paths straight (Proverbs 3:5-6).

Barbara Ferguson learns life lessons through everyday trials and triumphs. Her first book, *Life Beyond Cancer*, shares how God helped the young family through her husband's sickness and death. She is currently working on a book of poems to encourage senior citizens. This year she plans to publish *You're Not Too Old.*

Pearls of Truth

The Truth Setting Us Free

Beth Shriver

*T*he Son of Man has authority on earth to forgive sins (Luke 5:24).

I'm a guilt ridden person. You can make me feel shamed over the slightest offense. I'll take the blame and run with it. But I've come to realize that I'm giving the glory to Satan when I let guilt have free reign. He twists things around to get me thinking I made the mistake, and I should feel guilty about it. Then I start comparing my sins to others even though I know a sin is a sin; God doesn't grade on a curve. But how can He forgive some of the sins that people do? Is Jack the Ripper going to be sitting next to me in heaven if he repents?

It wasn't until I sat in a jail cell that I finally got forgiveness. Have you ever been in a jail? Walked through the metal detector, been frisked? Taken the elevator to the women's holding block? Heard the guards lock the doors behind you?

When I did prison ministry at a jail in downtown Dallas I learned what true forgiveness really is. Twelve of us walked into a large room, filled with twenty-four women who were incarcerated for various crimes. We sat facing them, and they were given the opportunity to tell their story, why they were there, what they did. Most of them participated, boldly telling us about their crime, and how long they'd been there, and when they were getting out. What amazed me was not the reason for them being there, but that each one became a Christian, or strengthened their relationship with Jesus while they were in jail. They received Christ's forgiveness!

What does it take to get some of us to where we need to be with Jesus? Hopefully not prison, but often it takes something that brings us to our knees? And when Jesus does open the cell door, do we forgive ourselves enough to walk out, or do we let Satan continue to tell us the lie that what we did can't be forgiven?

Faith Step: We are powerless to open the door until we ask for forgiveness, but when Jesus opens it will you take that first step to freedom?

Beth Shriver is the author of *Annie's Truth, Grace Given,* and *Healing Grace.* You can find her at *BethShriverWriter.com.*

How Can You Mend a Divided Heart?

Lisa Burkhardt Worley

When I watched the Cowboys-Giants season opener I had a dilemma. On one hand, I've followed the Cowboys since I was a little girl and covered them for many years as a sportscaster. On the other hand, I also have a special place in my heart for the Giants whom I reported on for several years, including broadcasting from their locker room after they won the 1991 Super Bowl against the Buffalo Bills. How do you root for two teams?

It's impossible. You have to choose. I realized this after I first went to work in New York City. I was asked by a sports producer if I was a Mets or a Yankees fan.

"I don't know. I kind of like them both," I replied.

"You can't follow both teams around here!" the producer exclaimed.

I found out there is no divided heart in sports!

We can't have a divided heart in our faith either. God wants us to be "all in" when it comes to our walk with Him. In Revelation 3:15-16, the Lord expresses His displeasure with the church at Laodicea for their wishy-washy faith, saying: *I know your deeds, that you are neither cold nor hot. I wish you were either one or the other! So, because you are lukewarm—neither hot nor cold—I am about to spit you out of my mouth.*

I don't ever want to be a bad taste in God's mouth do you?

How do we avoid sitting on the fence in our spiritual journey? First, we can turn our lives over to God and immerse ourselves in His word daily. We can also pray Psalm 86:11 over our lives: *Teach me your way, LORD, that I may rely on your faithfulness; give me an undivided heart, that I may fear your name.*

God wants us to have no other gods before Him. He desires to be the center of our lives, not on the periphery.

I pray that God is not disappointed when He looks at my heart. Avoiding a lukewarm faith is not as easy as picking a team. That's for sure.

By the way, I ended up pulling for the guys with the stars on their helmets. For me, there was no other choice, just like there is no other choice than a full-fledged, all-out devotion to God!

Lisa Burkhardt Worley is a former national television sports reporter, now Christian motivational speaker and writer and is the founder of Pearls of Promise Ministries, *pearlsofpromiseministries.com*. Visit the Pearls of Promise Facebook page: */pearlsofpromiseministries* or follow Lisa on Twitter *@pearlsofpromise*.

Hoarders

Rebecca Carrell

Don't store up treasures here on earth, where moths eat them and rust destroys them, and where thieves break in and steal (Matthew 6:19, NLT).

It takes about seven seconds for me to get sucked into a reality show. Pick a show—any show. No matter how bad it is, if I watch it for seven seconds, I'm hooked.

Fortunately, my schedule doesn't allow me to sit around and watch very often, but every now and then I find myself standing in front of the TV, remote control in hand, eyes wide and head shaking at what people are willing to reveal about themselves on television.

My most recent mouth-gaping-head-shaking experience? *Hoarders*.

If you haven't watched in horror along with me, *Hoarders* is a show that spotlights people with a legitimate mental-disorder. The first episode I viewed involved an elderly woman hoarding food. Her freezers, bursting at the seams, were duct-taped shut. She had two refrigerators (not uncommon) stuffed to the gills with rotting yogurt, cottage cheese, and any and every kind of perishable item you could imagine (highly uncommon). When her fridges could hold no more, she would stack fruit and vegetables anywhere she could find a square inch.

How many of us, in a spiritual sense, live the same way?

1 Peter 5:7: *Give all your worries and cares to God, for He cares for you* (NLT).

The human heart has a tendency to hoard. We hoard bitterness, resentment, unforgiveness, and jealousy. Some of us hoard grief, some of us, approval. Some hoard past accolades and achievements, while others, failures—clinging to past mistakes, unable to step out in faith for fear of repeating them.

What are you clinging to? Where do you store up your treasure?

I think of all the years I spent hoarding approval. Saying things I shouldn't say so people would listen to me. Not saying things I *should* say so that people wouldn't get mad at me. Filling my calendar with a never-ending stream of activities because I couldn't say no. Clinging to everything but Christ for security.

I couldn't experience true contentment until I allowed the Holy Spirit to come in and clean out my heart. With His Holy hazmat mask He cleared out resentment from past relationships. Disappointment from dreams not fulfilled. Fear of failure and the future. Alcoholism. Eating Disorders. He showed me that His is the only approval worth having, and then let me in on an astonishing truth: *But seek first the kingdom of God and His righteousness, and all these things will be added to you* (Matthew 6:33 ESV).

If we must hoard, let's hoard compassion, generosity, and loyalty. Let's store up a treasury of wisdom in our minds and love in our hearts. It's time to get *out* of our heads and into the game—to live by the power of the Holy Spirit, to walk by faith and not by sight!

Rebecca Ashbrook Carrell has been a radio personality in the Dallas Ft. Worth area since 1998. She left full-time radio to found LSS Ministries but can still be heard on a part-time basis at Christian talk station 90.9 KCBI. Rebecca writes and teaches Bible studies and authors a devotional on her website, *LoveServeShine.com.*

God Is Faithful; He Asks Us to Be Faithful

Janna Longfellow Hughes

Moreover it is required in stewards that one be found faithful (1 Corinthians 4:2, NKJV).

A hunger pang. I reached into my pocket and pulled out some cash. A snack wouldn't cost much. But, the money was needed for something else. Would I give in to misspending it now and maybe come up short later? I decided to be faithful to our family budget and hang onto the money.

I put the money away and prayed for God's provision. Before I left the produce area, a worker stacked up cases of ripe mangoes. He posted a sign that said the mangoes were specially priced. The offer allowed me to buy ripe mangoes and to still save the money budgeted for other things.

With the first bite, the bold flavors of mango burst in my mouth. Gratefully, I realized that by spending the entire amount earlier I would have short-circuited my little miracle and not tasted anything so delicious.

With the worldwide economy chafing, many of us choose to reevaluate the ways we've done things and take new directions. Many face greater obstacles than ever before.

In days of old, Joseph, son of Jacob, faced difficulties,

too. His brothers plotted to kill him. They sold him into slavery. A woman powerful enough to have him thrown into prison falsely accused him of rape. Even in prison he kept a good attitude.

The truth is Joseph remained faithful in difficult circumstances. Despite all of his troubles, God showed him grace and gave him favor in the prison warden's sight.

Everything Joseph did prospered. He was promoted to a prison supervisor and eventually to Chancellor of Egypt.

Once again, I relished the taste of the mango and the sweetness of God's provision. I felt glad He enabled me to remain faithful to His truth.

Father, when circumstances arise we cannot change, help us to be faithful stewards of all you've entrusted to us, knowing that you remain with us.

Janna Longfellow Hughes is a television producer and published writer who can be found at *JannaLongfellowHughes.com*. Janna has also written an ebook, *DEVELOP YOUR STORY - Tools for Building a Bridge to Your Audience* (download free at Janna's website).

Does God Still Give Us Signs?

Lisa Burkhardt Worley

The other day I was on the cell phone talking to my friend and co-author of our book, *If I Only Had...Following God's Path to Your Security*. Catherine had been praying about whether or not she was supposed to join our Pearls of Promise team and we were discussing that as well as a Bible study we are writing.

We continued our chat well after I arrived at my glamorous destination, the grocery store, so I eventually told Catherine I needed to go on in since I had been sitting in the car and the fruits and vegetables were waiting for me.

"Which grocery store are you at?" Catherine asked.

I told her, and as it turned out, she was also sitting in her car at the SAME supermarket parking lot. When we saw each other inside, we had a good laugh over the fact that we could have been talking face to face if we'd known we were gabbing a few yards from each other!

As she reflected on the "coincidence", Catherine later realized it was God's way of telling her the two of us were on the same path with the same destination, and that it made sense to join Pearls of Promise as creative director.

But did God really give Catherine a sign?

Some would argue that God did not, based on Matthew 16:4 where Jesus tells the Pharisees and Sadducees, *A wicked and adulterous generation looks for a miraculous sign, but none will be given it except the sign of Jonah.* He puts an exclamation point on that statement by immediately walking away after he said it.

When I first saw that verse, my thought was, "I will never ask God for a sign because I don't want to be labeled wicked!" I found myself muttering, "I want God's direction but I'm not going to ask for a sign; nope not me. I don't need a sign."

However, when you peruse the entire passage, you realize the Pharisees and Sadducees had missed countless miracles of God working through Jesus. He had just fed four thousand with seven loaves of bread and two fish. Prior to that, He healed countless people with disabilities who responded by praising the God of Israel once they were whole again.

Weren't those signs?

According to the *MacArthur Bible Commentary*,* the Pharisees and Sadducees wanted "a miraculous work of cosmological proportions, like the rearranging of the constellations" something more than a yawner like casting out a demon, which they had just witnessed.

They had missed the signs!

That's why Jesus was so upset, and probably threw up His hands when He walked away.

So the answer to the question, "Does God still give us signs?" is "YES!" However, a sign may not come in the package you imagined. It's important to be open to God's creative direction.

What about you? Do you believe God still gives us signs?

*MacArthur, John, *The MacArthur Bible Commentary*. Nashville: Thomas Nelson, Inc., 2005.

Lisa Burkhardt Worley is a former national television sports reporter, now Christian motivational speaker and writer, and is the founder of Pearls of Promise Ministries, *pearlsofpromiseministries.com*. She is the co-author of the award winning manuscript, *If I Only Had...Following God's Path to Your Security* and holds a Masters of Theological Studies Degree from Perkins School of Theology.

Inside Out or Outside In

Catherine Weiskopf

If I speak in the tongues of men or of angels, but do not have love, I am only a resounding gong or a clanging cymbal. If I have the gift of prophecy and can fathom all mysteries and all knowledge, and if I have a faith that can move mountains, but do not have love, I am nothing. If I give all I possess to the poor and give over my body to hardship that I may boast, but do not have love, I gain nothing (1 Corinthians 13:1-3).

You see a friend's tag on the back of their shirt, the shirt seams run up the side, the color is faded. "Honey, your top is on inside out," you warn her as she blushes.

Shirts, socks, pants, they should all be worn outside in, but how should your life be lived, outside in or inside out?

Before you answer, let me confess. I've been living my life outside in. This means I do the right things most of the time. I help a friend in need; I donate money to worthy causes; I take meals to people; I teach Sunday school; I help people in the neighborhood. I appear on the outside to be a good Christian woman.

But on the inside, it's not pretty. Jealousy often grabs me and won't let go for days. I have trouble forgetting the simplest of slights by a friend. When someone wrongs my child I could carry around the thoughts of revenge for years. Interrupt me when I'm on an idea and I'll ignore you, I promise.

I think, though I hate to admit it, I have something in common with the most dreaded and shunned people in the Bible: the Pharisees.

The Pharisees were constantly raked over the coals by Jesus. They are also our examples of how to live outside in. They knew all the rules; they spent their lives studying them; they had a list of "shoulds" even longer than mine. But what did Jesus say about their hearts? Matthew 15:8 says: *These people honor me with their lips, but their hearts are far from me.*

So how did I get here in their prickly company?

By worrying more about the state of my image than the state of my heart.

By paying more attention to my "shoulds" than the heart of Jesus.

So no charity points for the time I cooked a meal for my neighbors but resented it the whole time. And the time I took all my son's friends to youth group but fumed the whole time was a loss. God doesn't keep track of good deeds. There is not a brownie point counter in heaven, but God is carefully watching and working on our hearts—mine especially.

Dear God, Help me to live inside out. Give me your love for people so that my reasons for helping flow from love.

Catherine Weiskopf is creative director of Pearls of Promise Ministries and is one of the editors for the *Pearls of Promise* devotional. She is a regular contributor to the Pearls of Promise blog and can be found on Twitter *@Cweiskopf.*

Fragrance Free

Lisa Burkhardt Worley

I recently developed a severe allergy I could not explain. Periodically my eyes would swell up, develop bright red rings around them and then redness would cover my face and neck. I looked like one of the characters from the movie Night of the Living Dead. It wasn't a good look!

So after about four bouts with this reaction, I went to the dermatologist to get to the bottom of it. After some allergy testing, I discovered I was highly allergic to two things, rubber and fragrance. If I touched either one, then rubbed my eyes, I risked transforming into something that no longer looked human.

So I left, disappointed about the fragrance allergy because everything I used to primp had a sweet smell! I decided to be more careful about touching my eyes, but did not make the commitment to give up my fragrance-laced products.

My decision to hold onto all of the cosmetics I loved dearly was not a wise one. One week later, the frightening face reappeared. At that point I understood how The Hulk felt when he transformed so quickly from a normal human to a monster, and I headed to the doctor again.

"Are you still using your products with fragrance?" she asked me bluntly.

I sheepishly admitted I was. She told me in order to avoid any further outbreaks I had to totally give up every ounce of makeup, shampoo and hair spray I use and replace them with fragrance free items.

"What? I have to stop wearing the mascara I've faithfully coated my lashes with for twenty years? I can no longer spritz my hair for frizz control?" I shuddered at the thought of my "hard to tame" blond locks without it. However, this time I listened, and threw out all the old and replaced it with new, fragrance free items.

As I reflect on this scenario, I think of our lives as Christians. When we first accept Christ, 2 Corinthians 5:17 says, *Therefore, if anyone is in Christ, he is a new creation; the old has gone, the new has come!* But oftentimes, even after becoming a believer, we still hold onto some of the old, don't we? Because of that, we can't quite live the fruitful, abundant life Christ promises. If we don't give up some of our old, bad habits, sin creeps in, and eventually takes over completely like an irritating rash that spreads. We then wonder, "How did this happen?" "Why am I such a mess?" That's when we need to do a soul search to figure out what is causing the nasty outbreak in our lives. Maybe we have to remove something from our world that doesn't line up with God's word, so we have total healing.

Unfortunately, I still have a little redness under my eyes, but I realized I had not replaced my under eye concealer. I was still holding onto one last product, but plan to replace the last of the irritants this week for a complete transformation.

I know I am guilty of holding onto one or two sins as well. You may also have an area you have not given up to God. If that's so, it's still not God's best for you. Pray that you have the strength to overcome, so you can release your grasp on whatever is irritating you.

In my case, even though I will soon be fragrance-free, I know obedience in my Christian walk still emits a pleasing aroma to God!

Lisa Burkhardt Worley is a former national television sports reporter, now Christian motivational speaker and writer and is the founder of Pearls of Promise Ministries, *pearlsofpromiseministries.com*. She is the co-author of the award winning manuscript, *If I Only Had...Following God's Path to Your Security* and is an editor for the *Pearls of Promise* devotional. Follow her on Twitter *@pearlsofpromise*.

My Lifeline

Jan Deering

A number of years ago, God impressed upon me the importance of being in His Word on a daily basis. I have found that God's Word is truly my lifeline. After all, God's Word is His love letter to each of us.

Psalm 19:7-10 says ...

The instructions of the Lord are perfect ...

The decrees of the Lord are trustworthy...

The commandments of the Lord are right...

The laws of the Lord are true; each one is fair. (NLT)

This is why I run to His Word each morning—it's perfect, trustworthy, right, and reliable...

I often start my quiet time with the words of Psalm 25:4 & 5:

Show me your ways, LORD, teach me your paths.

Guide me in your truth and teach me, for you are God my Savior, and my hope is in you all day long.

If we allow Him, He will show us His path where we should go. And He will point out the right road for us to walk, for He is faithful. And if we put Jesus in the center of every day—every moment will be for His glory and for building up His kingdom.

Proverbs 16:9 says, *We can make our plans, but the LORD determines our steps* (NLT).

Give each day to the Lord. Surrender your plans to His will and He will be faithful to direct your steps to accomplish what He wants you to accomplish, to say the words that He wants you to say, to live your day glorifying Him.

Jan Deering is a women's ministry founder, retreat coordinator, prayer committee coordinator, Bible study facilitator, a coordinator of various large group meals, vendor coordinator of annual craft show and a certified spiritual director.

Walking Jewel

Lisa Burkhardt Worley

I took off on my morning walk this morning and had just left my driveway when I heard the pitter patter of rapid steps behind me. Worried it was someone's loose dog, I zipped my head around and saw someone's loose dog alright, mine! Our dog, Jewel, had once again escaped through a hole under our fence, and wanted to join me on my morning trek around the neighborhood.

She cowered as she looked up at me with that cute doggie smile, knowing inside she had achieved a great feat by catching up to me, but there were still consequences for the breakout. She was sent off to solitary confinement in the laundry room so I didn't have to worry about another escape. Being merciful, I promised to walk her after I returned.

There's a reason I don't take Jewel out on the leash that much. It is work. Even several sessions with a local dog whisperer did not teach us how to keep her from pulling us around the block rather than leading her. I am generally a walker, but I learned it is better to run with Jewel so she is not gagging on the leash and the ligaments in my arm aren't being stretched beyond reason. When I put the leash on her collar, she starts to gag before we even leave the house and we haven't moved yet! I guess she's conditioned herself to believe that's just what you do when you're on a leash.

As I'm trying to keep up with Jewel, it occurred to me that our relationship with the Lord is often like my "walk" with Jewel. We race off in a direction that is not of God rather than let Him lead us. We are an impatient people and want things to happen now. We tug and pull and gag when it would be so much more pleasant if we walked side by side with God at His pace.

My goal each morning is to ask the Lord to order my steps, and because I do tend to want things to happen faster than they do most of the time, I find the words of Psalm 143:7-8 work well as a prayer:

Answer me quickly, LORD; my spirit fails. Do not hide your face from me or I will be like those who go down to the pit. Let the morning bring me word of your unfailing love, for I have put my trust in you. Show me the way I should go, for to you I entrust my life.

My dog, Jewel, will probably always pull me on our walks together but we don't always have to pull God! Our daily walk with Him won't be so strained if we let Him guide us.

Lisa Burkhardt Worley is a former national television sports reporter, now Christian motivational speaker and writer and is the founder of Pearls of Promise Ministries, *pearlsofpromiseministries.com*. She is the co-author of the award winning manuscript, *If I Only Had...Following God's Path to Your Security* and is an editor for the *Pearls of Promise* devotional.

God's Word Is the Truth

Lisa Mick

I speak the truth in Christ—I am not lying, my conscience confirms it through the Holy Spirit (Romans 9:1).

God often calls upon me to tell the truth to others even when it hurts them. It's very hard for me to believe God uses me in this way. At times, I will sit and converse with Him; "Are you sure? God, that is going to hurt them, I don't want to tell them." Then He gives me a scripture like Romans 9:1 to convince me it is true. I always use Christ's name and my conscience definitely confirms it through the Holy Spirit because it will not leave my mind until I speak it to the individual.

He knows how much I love His people, and He knows how hard this is for me to do. Often when I tell them what He has impressed upon my heart, He will have already given them the same message. This confirms His will for them. You can imagine the relief I feel. *Imploring us with much urgency that we would receive the gift and the fellowship of the ministering to the saints* (2 Corinthians 8:4, NKJV)

What joy this is. How wonderful our Father is to provide me with the TRUTH in His Word.

Do you have a spiritual gift that you feel uncomfortable using? He wants me to share with you how important it is to receive whatever gift He has given you. Listen to your counselor inside, because He placed it in you to guide you. One of my purposes here on Earth is to minister His truth to His people. Even though it is hard, I am always blessed because I discern the truth and follow what He calls me to do. Obeying the Father always brings great reward, favor and blessings.

So my friend, what is your gift? Have you searched His Word to find it? I promise you if you search with all your heart, He will answer that search as He has for me. When you are in His perfect will, life is grand dear one. His perfect will for you is truth and you will only find that in His Word. A dear friend told me as my walk with Christ was growing, His Word works. Amen.

Then you will know the truth, and the truth will set you free (John 8:32).

Lisa Mick is director of outreach for Pearls of Promise Ministries and is one of the editors for the *Pearls of Promise* devotional. Lisa is also co-authoring a Bible study designed to help non-writers record their faith journey. She is a regular contributor to the Pearls of Promise blog and can be found on Twitter *@LisaGMick*.

Pearls of Wisdom

The Teachable Wisdom of Zig Ziglar

Krish Dhanam

In the year 2005 on the 24th of March I watched my hero and mentor, Zig Ziglar, finish a talk in Mumbai, India. I'd worked hard to bring this giant of personal development to the land of my birth. Here was the culmination of one of my biggest dreams, but the best lesson was about to be revealed.

In an unscripted moment he announced to the gathering that he would no longer travel internationally and that India would be his final overseas venture.

Caught off guard, I queried Mr. Ziglar at dinner that night before his return flight to the US. In his unmistakable deep Southern drawl, he said he had contemplated lightening his schedule for a while and international travel would be the first to be curbed. I agreed with the sentiment, but wondered why he had chosen India to make the announcement.

His answer was one of incredible wisdom. He told me he watched with fascination how hard I had worked so I could show him off to my native land. His humble belief was if I knew this was just a formality before retirement, then I would somehow think he was just going through the motions. He wanted me to be excited that the executives of India would receive a well thought out and orchestrated message. He had waited to make this announcement because he was most concerned about the satisfaction I would derive from achieving one of my own goals.

I have learned many lessons from Mr. Ziglar but the most important one was to always be other people focused. Another wise man, Fred Smith, Sr., said that humility is not thinking less of yourself but less often of yourself. That day in Mumbai the ever wise Zig Ziglar thought more of my dreams and goals and less about his plans.

"You can have everything in life you want if you just help enough other people get what they want." Zig Ziglar

But the wisdom that is from above is first pure, then peaceable, gentle, willing to yield, full of mercy and good fruits, without partiality and without hypocrisy (James 3:17, NKJV).

Krish Dhanam is the author of *The American Dream from an Indian Heart* and *From Abstracts to Absolutes*. His websites are *krishdhanam.com* and *malaministries.org*.

The House of Cards

Catherine Weiskopf

The devil is the father of lies. When he tells lies he speaks his own language. God is the God of truth (John 8:43-45).

I am struck by an image as I read these words in my Bible. I am standing with a house of cards around me. Each card is labeled with a lie. The cards are only paper but inside on a calm sunny day I feel safe because I don't see the truth about the flimsiness of the structure.

The biggest lie in the house of cards, that I have lived with most of my life, is "I am not enough."

I have based my existence on proving that this lie isn't true. Putting up card after card has made my house larger and more vulnerable to falling. The cards, each labeled with a way to "prove" my worth, go up around me:

One card with a heart says, "If people love me more than you I am worthy." I look for invites to prove that people like me and I'm ok. If I have an active social life, I am loved and my house stands.

One with a diamond says, "If I look better than others, then I am worthy." It's hard to be around pretty people because it makes me aware of my own unattractiveness and shakes my building.

One with a club says, "If I am nice to everyone and do whatever they ask, then I am worthy." When people compliment others about how nice they are when I'm around, my house wavers.

One with a spade says, "If I work hard and accomplish

more than others, then I am worthy." I work my fingers to the bone and want acknowledgement.

And so I spend my time proving that my unworthiness isn't true, but I do it with other lies.

But underneath the card of lies, underneath me, is a table on which everything stands. The table, in my vision, is labeled as Jesus. Jesus with one puff of air blows the house of cards down and then I look around and see the truth. The truth is I must have Christ's mind with the matter of my worth.

For you created my inmost being; you knit me together in my mother's womb.

I praise you because I am fearfully and wonderfully made; your works are wonderful,

I know that full well (Psalm 139:13-14).

I am worthy and my worth comes from Him. The house of cards that surrounded me for so long has not been keeping me safe, rather it has prevented me from seeing His truth.

Dear God, I know oftentimes lies seem like the truth; help me to know the truth, and help me to see that lies are a house of cards.

Catherine Weiskopf is creative director of Pearls of Promise Ministries. She is the author of math books for elementary Students: *Lemon & Ice & Everything Nice* from Scholastic and co-author of the cartoon illustrated *Adventures in Mathopolis* series. Check out her books at *cweiskopf.com*.

Do Unto Others

Jennifer Mersberger

As a child, I grew up hearing the Golden Rule, *Do unto others what you would have them do to you.* So I thought as long as I was a good person and tried not to do hurtful things I would be fine, right? Boy was I wrong.

It didn't take long to realize how hard the Golden Rule was to live by. Life became unfair and people showed they could be cruel. It became more and more difficult for me to do good things when I was being treated badly. There was a constant battle between what I should do and what I wanted to do.

Fortunately, God doesn't expect us to be good all on our own. He promises that when we stay in close relationship with Him, He will give us the strength to do what we can't do alone:

Love the unlovable.

Forgive those who hurt us.

Do good things for people who may not deserve it.

Our goodness comes from Him, it's His love poured out through us. When we abide in the Lord, His thoughts become our thoughts. His ways become our ways. We become more and more like Christ as we allow His love and power to live in us through the Holy Spirit.

Believer, our goodness does not come from our ability to be good. Our goodness comes from the One who is nothing but good. He equips us to do good works.

He doesn't ask us to give Him our best effort, He asks us to give Him our heart.

I am the vine; you are the branches. If you remain in me and I in you, you will bear much fruit; apart from me you can do nothing (John 15:5).

Jennifer Mersberger is an Amazon Top 15 Christian author, public speaker, and founder of Lamplight Ministry. Through her Bible studies and weekly blog, Jennifer uses her unique perspective and fun sense of humor to help you see God in your everyday. Get to know her at *lamplightministry.com* and *Facebook.com/JenniferMersberger*.

Falling Leaves of Humility

Mary Jane Downs

While raking leaves, I began to ponder their colors. When the leaves came out in the spring, they were a lush green. Now the leaves sported red, yellow, and orange as their attire. These colors are the leaves' best work before falling to rest on the ground.

Unexpectedly, I felt my attention drawn to the pile of brown leaves I was raking. My curiosity peaked.

"Lord, why do all the leaves turn brown? Why don't they retain their color?"

"Brown symbolizes humility. After a season of glory, everything has to come back to the place of humility. That is the way I keep things in perspective. That is also how I help you from losing your perspective," he responded to my spirit.

Yes, there are good times when I grow in my faith. I am able to venture out and maybe even accomplish a great feat or two. His mercy and grace are with me. I am able to witness to others. But then slowly, everything comes to an end. The signs of a changing season begin. What used to work does not work anymore. God is letting me know the present season is over. It's time to come back to rest, reflect, and rejuvenate at the foot of the cross to humble myself before Him.

What does it mean to be humble? Humility is acknowledging that I am totally dependent on God. It is God who sustains me and brings me through all situations whether I recognize Him or not.

While I am following my God-given directives, my focus can so easily be twisted from working *with* God to working *for* God. Working *with* God, I seek for and strive to walk in godly wisdom. Working *for* God, I tend to do what I think is best. My decisions become centered on human reasoning. The result of my change of focus may not show up right away. Eventually, I face the issue of pride, humility's adversary.

The best way to handle pride is at the foot of the cross and focus on scriptures like Psalm 16:8: *I have set the Lord always before me because He is at my right hand. I shall not be moved* (NKJV). God is always willing and ready to support us with abundant grace and a renewed focus on Him. Humility will not be able to rise again until I deal with the issue of my pride. Once I have regained my focus on God, I will be ready to bloom again.

Where are you in your walk? Are you walking *with* God or *for* God? If pride has sidetracked you, don't worry. God is there to help you find your way back. It will take some time before the throne of grace and a willingness to seek godly counsel. But when you are ready to stand, you will be refreshed and refocused to serve our Savior again.

Mary Jane Downs is an author, speaker and teacher who lives in the foothills of the Asheville Mountains. Her website is *maryjanewrites.com*.

Life Lessons from Canoeing

Lisa Burkhardt Worley

Over the summer, my husband and I went canoeing with family members down the Pere Marquette River near Ludington, Michigan. My husband and I are novices at canoeing so we ran into trouble more times than I'd like to admit. We capsized twice; one time I hit the back of my head on a large tree branch. I don't know what my body found in the other mishap, but it resulted in bruises up and down my left leg. I thought of Jesus' words, in John 16:33: *In this world you will have trouble...*

As I reflect back on our trip, I realize there were many life lessons we can learn from canoeing!

It took us two hours to understand this, but when canoeing, you must anticipate the problems ahead and begin paddling well before the current has a chance to overtake you. I realized that's a life lesson. When we spot temptation or a compromising situation ahead, do we steer clear of it before the current is too strong to resist?

The next lesson I learned is: sometimes in life we will get bonked on the head, and there is nothing we can do about it. Our canoe was headed straight for a mammoth tree branch that sat six inches off the water. When my husband yelled, "Duck!" I knew there was no avoiding hitting my head because I couldn't bend low enough to prevent the collision. Life is that way, right? Sometimes there is no avoiding a bonk in the head.

1 Peter 4:12-13 says, *Dear friends, do not be surprised at the fiery ordeal that has come on you to test you, as though something strange were happening to you. But rejoice inasmuch as you participate in the sufferings of Christ, so that you may be overjoyed when His glory is revealed.* Didn't Christ also suffer on a tree?

Because I was in the front of the canoe, I wasn't supposed to steer the vessel. I only paddled when my husband told me to. I had to trust him to guide us down the river, which turned out to be difficult for me as I would try to "help us out" every so often. Therein is the third lesson. In life, God is in the back of our canoe and we must trust Him to steer us because He knows the stretches and bends of our life river and He sees the difficulties we are unaware of yet.

If God had been in the back of our canoe on the Pere Marquette, rather than my husband, would we have still toppled into the river twice? I want to say, "no," but sometimes God allows setbacks to draw us nearer to Him and to teach us a few lessons, all preparation for that final canoe ride to eternity. *In this world you will have trouble. But take heart! I have overcome the world.*

Lisa Burkhardt Worley is a former national television sports reporter, now Christian motivational speaker and writer and is the founder of Pearls of Promise Ministries, *pearlsofpromiseministries.com.* She is the co-author of the award winning manuscript, *If I Only Had...Following God's Path to Your Security* and is co-authoring a Bible study about how God takes you out of the world to do the unpopular. Lisa is an editor for the *Pearls of Promise* devotional.

Seasoned With Salt and Grace

Mary Ann Springer Moore

Have you ever responded to a text or email without thinking it through? Or written an email out of anger just to get it off your chest then accidentally hit send instead of trash? Yikes. The day of fast conversations are here; we can text, email, tweet, and Facebook without taking time to consider what we are saying and then the damage is done.

Today, during my quiet time, I got a text addressing an issue that is my "passion," she held the opposite viewpoint which made my insides churn. Of course, being the godly Christian woman I am, I quickly responded so I could correct her wrong thinking. I really just wanted to give her a piece of my mind but I can't give too much away. I don't have much to lose! Literally, as I was finishing the text, this Bible verse, Colossians 4:6, was texted to me: *Let your conversation be always full of grace, seasoned with salt, so that you may know how to answer everyone.* I laugh out loud. God has phenomenal timing!

My words were seasoned with way too much salt. Salt is a good seasoning, but too much of it ruins the taste and is bad for our health. As I reread my text, I saw the bitterness in it and what harm it would do.

In Matthew 5:13 Jesus reminds us, *You are the salt of the earth.* But we must always let our words and our conversations be seasoned with grace. God's word is what stopped the pouring of this salt shaker; it tenderized my heart, cleansed my thinking and pre-served a friendship.

So the next time trouble comes knocking at your door, look at the bigger picture and ask, "How can I handle this situation with both salt and grace?" Go to the God of all wisdom and ask for His direction; He promises to guide and direct you. Respond in humility, for that is the character God wants to create in us. Oh and next time you get a prompting to send a Bible verse to someone, just do it, you may be the very instrument God uses to help them!

Mary Ann Springer Moore is a Christian motivational speaker in Northern California. She has led Bible study groups for 18 years and enjoys working with teens. She is currently enrolled at Golden Gate Baptist Theological Seminary.

Revealing Results in Healing

Karen Ambler

W hen I was a kid I was a bit of a wild child, definitely a tomboy, heavy on the "boy." Always climbing, running, jumping, breaking, pounding, basically not sitting still long enough to catch my breath! As a result of my exuberance, injuries were a big part of my life. Among those injuries, was the oft-received and always dreaded splinter. For me, that was the worst kind of wound.

Normally I'd take bumps and bruises in stride, but along with the splinter came the need to have it pulled out. Forgive me for the stereotype, but here is where I was *all girl*. Can you say, "Drama Queen?" Mom used to say I could have won an Oscar for my performances during the "extractions." Mom, doing her best impression of a python, would have to literally hold me down. Dad had the even less desirable role of chief surgeon or octopus! He'd grasp a sterilized straight pin in one hand, and with the other he'd attempt to hold my arm, or hand, or leg still enough to get a grip on the end of the offending hunk of wood. And I would scream like they were killing me!

Not wanting to experience that trauma again, one day I decided to let a small splinter alone and leave it unreported. I hid it from Mom and Dad, trying hard to conceal my wincing face when I'd catch it on something. The natural course of events took place, and it became infected, swollen, tender, and raging red!

When I could no longer hold a pencil or fork, I sheepishly presented the infected finger to mom. Since I had chosen to let it go unresolved for so long, it was now beyond my parents' abilities to fix and we had to see the pediatrician. Suffice to say it was not pretty and extremely painful to have excised from my finger that which began as a tiny splinter.

We all have life's "splinters" but isn't it vastly better to present them to God when they first occur, rather than wait till infection ensues? I've had strongholds that started out as small issues, but after I hid them for years, grew into dangerous life-altering infections. But be encouraged! God is full of mercy and grace and is incomparably the best surgeon! Here is what the Bible says about the effectiveness of God's Word in this type of surgery: *For we do not have a high priest who is unable to empathize with our weaknesses, but we have one who has been tempted in every way, just as we are—yet He did not sin. Let us then approach God's throne of grace with confidence, so that we may receive mercy and find grace to help us in our time of need* (Hebrews 4:12-16).

No offense to my dad, but this beats his tweezers any day! God already knows the splinter is there anyway, and He knows how it got there, so you might as well tell Him about it. No one heals like the Father does and, no one loves you more either.

Karen Ambler's passion is helping women discover their true identity in Christ and find freedom through His Word. Karen mentors and leads Bible studies through her home-based ministry "For The Joy." She also ministers to hurting people with her registered therapy dog, Bendito, through Blessed Be Animal Assisted Therapy. Contact Karen at *blessedbeforthejoy.com*.

The Goal Is the Fruit

Mary Jane Downs

This past summer, I grew a couple of tomato and pepper plants in pots because I love BLT sandwiches and fresh toppings for my mini pizzas. When the plants matured to the point of having flowers and producing small fruit, I felt the Holy Spirit ask me to look at the fruit on the vine more carefully. It was then that I noticed *'the flower came before the fruit.'* I asked the Holy Spirit to explain.

He began to show me the mental picture of the flower/tomato on the vine again. Then I heard the Holy Spirit say: *That is where you are right now...The bearing of the fruit.*

I received Jesus as my Savior at a young age. From there, I struggled with what it meant for Jesus to be Lord over my life. Even though I was growing in the knowledge of God, I still felt defeated all the time. I tried for years to do the right thing to earn God's favor and respect but all the while feeling like a failure.

Finally, I understood what the grace of God really meant. I also began to accept Christ's leadership. The more I studied and meditated on scripture, the more I relaxed in his arms, and slowly but surely, I began handing over every aspect of my life to Him.... trusting Jesus to direct my paths.

The tomato plant, root system, leaves, and finally the budding flower all represent different aspects of my growth in Christ. The developing flower symbolizes the lordship of Christ over all areas of my life. The final fading of the flower represents my total surrender to develop Christ-likeness in my life.

The scripture that keeps popping up is:

I have been crucified with Christ. It is no longer I who live, but Christ who lives in me. And the life I now live in the flesh I live by faith in the Son of God, who loved me and gave Himself for me (Galatians 2:20, ESV).

Where are you in your walk with Christ? Are you a new member of the family or have you been a fellow believer for a while? Wherever you are, there is always something new to grasp that will bring more confidence and freedom to your life. I challenge you to keep seeking Christ so your fruit can come to full maturity.

Mary Jane Downs is an author, speaker and teacher who lives in the foothills of the Asheville Mountains. Her website is *maryjanewrites.com*.

Spotlight or Lamp

Catherine Weiskopf

You are the light of the world. A town built on a hill cannot be hidden (Matthew 5:14).

When God asks us to be the light of the world which light does He mean? I asked myself this question as I gazed at the different lights around my house: a glaring spotlight in our backyard, a laser pointer I used for presentations, energy saving LED light that illuminates from overhead, or a soft glowing living room lamp.

I was thinking about these lights while I talked to my sister one day. "Mom doesn't understand how I can talk to Andrea because she left her husband," my sister said. "But I don't want to judge her."

Her words were a laser focused right on my guilty heart. Two neighbors had dumped their husbands and found new boyfriends. How should I treat them? Like a spotlight pointing out to everyone what they were doing wrong? Or a confused motion sensitive nightlight that went off instead of on when they were around?

My sister continued with a story of another woman ostracized because of her affair. "Her family isn't talking to her," she said. "When they see her, they ignore her."

"That's terrible," I said, feeling the poor woman's pain. What followed can only be described as the great throat clearing from the sky. "Ahem," followed by, "Does this sound familiar?"

Yes, that's what I was doing, ostracizing people

because of their behavior. I saw them at the bus stop everyday and didn't say a word. I thought what they were doing was awful and thought they were awful for doing it. And as long as I'm being honest, I had slipped into talking about their awful behavior. Plain and simple, I'd taken on the role of being the great spotlight in the sky.

The Bible is full of advice about judgment. Jesus Himself cleared a street of spotlighters with the simple phrase: *Let any one of you who is without sin be the first to throw a stone at her* (John 8:7).

I wondered how I should handle the bus stop. Since a spotlight was out, what kind of light should I be?

A day later, shopping, I saw a gorgeous lamp. A light bulb set between two brass ornate pieces—the base and the top. Surrounding the bulb were strings of crystals. The light this lamp gave off reminded me of the broken bits of rays I see when the sun breaks through a cloud.

God wanted me to be the light that breaks through the clouds and darkness: light that is warm, heavenly, and shining from within, outwards. Shining my light meant being with people in the mess. God didn't want me to shine my light onto a situation; He wanted me to shine my light into their lives.

Dear God, Help me to be your light in the darkness. Help me to be a loving, healing and warm light, drawing all to you.

Catherine Weiskopf is creative director of Pearls of Promise Ministries. She is the author of Math Books for Elementary Students: *Lemon & Ice & Everything Nice* from Scholastic and co-author of the cartoon illustrated *Adventures in Mathopolis* series. Check out her books at *cweiskopf.com.*

Without Bad You Wouldn't Know Good

Lisa Burkhardt Worley

Recently I visited a woman going through a difficult stretch. "Nothing good has happened to me in the last 18 years," she said as soon as I sat down.

"Nothing good?" I asked and then prompted her on her children's health.

"Oh yes, they're great!" she answered.

"Is that not good?" I pointed out. "Do you like the church you attend?"

"Yes, I love it," she said.

"Isn't that good?"

I am not downplaying this woman's situation in any way. I acknowledge that she has been through a lot of "bad" but I believe in anyone's life, there is good. I also believe without bad, we would not recognize the good.

God never promised us life would be perfect or that nothing bad would happen. In fact, Jesus is upfront about this in John 16:33 when He says, *In this world you will have trouble...* However, as I look back at all the worst periods of trouble in my own life, I realize they were also the greatest periods of spiritual growth.

Because of the untimely death of my father two

months before I was born, I suffered the consequences of his death throughout my childhood but if he had not died, I am not sure I would have ever known or accepted the love of my Father in heaven. Through a devastating job loss, I rededicated my life to Christ, and after a family trial a few years ago, I became more intentional about intercessory prayer and continue to see incredible results from my commitment to daily prayer on my knees.

When I was going through my most recent difficult stretch, I talked to a good friend about the struggle I was going through and she asked, "What do you think God wants you to learn from this?" I have never forgotten her words and I ask that question when things get "bad." Usually there is a lesson to learn.

Call me a Pollyanna but because of past experience, I know that good will eventually emerge from the bad, which falls in line with the promise of Romans 8:28 when the Apostle Paul states, *And we know that in all things God works for the good of those who love Him, who have been called according to His purpose.* When we trust these words, we will always wait in anticipation for the good to be revealed and that alone will help us see beyond the valley we are in. Good is just beyond the horizon.

Lisa Burkhardt Worley is a former national television sports reporter, now Christian motivational speaker and writer and is the founder of Pearls of Promise Ministries, *pearlsofpromiseministries.com*. She holds a Masters of Theological Studies degree from Perkins School of Theology and is the co-author of the award winning manuscript, *If I Only Had... Following God's Path to Your Security.*

About the Compilers

Lisa Burkhardt Worley is a former national television sports reporter, who now reaches women through her speaking and writing ministry that she founded, Pearls of Promise. She loves her sisters in Christ and has been called by God to help women grow in their faith and overcome their strongholds. Lisa appeared on HBO's *Inside the NFL,* ESPN, the Madison Square Garden Network and locally at WTVC-TV in Chattanooga, TN, and KENS-TV in San Antonio, TX. She blogs regularly and co-authored the award winning manuscript, *If I Only Had...Following God's Path to Your Security* and the Bible study, *The UnCrowd: How God Calls Us Out of the World to Do the Unpopular,* which is currently being taught at churches in North Texas. Lisa holds a Bachelor's Degree from Texas Lutheran University and a Masters of Theological Studies degree from Perkins School of Theology. Lisa has been married for over 27 years to Jeff and has two children, Kyle and Bret.

Lisa Mick is the director of outreach for Pearls of Promise Ministries. Lisa says, "I've been praying for two years to be of service to the Father." She has a large heart for women and possesses an enthusiastic personality that adds warmth and love to the ministry. Lisa has served in many ministry leadership positions ranging from being a Sunday school and Vacation Bible School teacher to a Meals on Wheels delivery driver and Meals on Wheels cook. Lisa currently serves on the First Friday Feast Team at Trietsch Memorial United Methodist

Church. She is co-authoring a book designed to help non-writers record their faith journey and also writes devotions for the Pearls of Promise Ministries website. Lisa has been married for 25 years to Dennis and has two children, Brandon and Barrett.

Catherine Weiskopf is the Creative Director for Pearls of Promise Ministries. Catherine Weiskopf says, "For as long as I can remember, God has used my writing to heal me and encourage others." Catherine, author of three published books, most recently co-authored the award winning manuscript, *If I Only Had... Following God's Path to Your Security.* Catherine also co-authored a Bible study, *The Un-Crowd: How God Calls Us Out of the World to Do the Unpopular* and is working on a book designed to help non-writers record their faith journey. Catherine has been married for 25 years to Arthur and has two children, Ben and Holly.

Pearls of Promise Ministries is dedicated to helping women find freedom in Christ. In light of our mission ten percent of the proceeds from the sale of the *Pearls of Promise* devotional will be donated to "Disrupt Human Trafficking" (*DisruptHT.org*). "Disrupt Human Trafficking" is a 501c3 nonprofit organization that provides no cost advanced law enforcement training to international law enforcement agencies, prosecutors, and nongovernmental agencies for the purpose of teaching investigative skills to disrupt and dismantle human trafficking criminal organizations.